Isabelle Duquesne

# Schools as Zones of Peace in Nepal

# Studies on Education

Volume 4

LIT

Isabelle Duquesne

# Schools as Zones of Peace in Nepal

## The Impact of Peace Education on Social Equity, Good Governance and Sustainable Economic Development in Post-Conflict Societies

Applying the PEACE formula $B3.i3^2$

LIT

Cover photo: Isabelle Duquesne, 2015

**Bibliographic information published by the Deutsche Nationalbibliothek**
The Deutsche Nationalbibliothek lists this publication in the Deutsche Nationalbibliografie; detailed bibliographic data are available on the Internet at http://dnb.d-nb.de.

ISBN 978-3-643-90823-0

**A catalogue record for this book is available from the British Library**


Klosbachstr. 107
CH-8032 Zürich
Tel. +41 (0) 44-251 75 05
E-Mail: zuerich@lit-verlag.ch http://www.lit-verlag.ch

**Distribution:**

In the UK: Global Book Marketing, e-mail: mo@centralbooks.com
In North America: International Specialized Book Services, e-mail: orders@isbs.com
In Germany: LIT Verlag Fresnostr. 2, D-48159 Münster
Tel. +49 (0) 2 51-620 32 22, Fax +49 (0) 2 51-922 60 99, e-mail: vertrieb@lit-verlag.de

In Austria: Medienlogistik Pichler-ÖBZ, e-mail: mlo@medien-logistik.at
e-books are available at www.litwebshop.de

## Editorial note

The word “PACE” in the formula *PACE = B3.i3*$^2$ refers to the Italian word which means “peace”. Emblazoned in bold on the background of a rainbow, the PACE flag was first used in Italy at a peace march in 1961. It became popular during the anti-nuclear weapons demonstrations across Europe. In 2002, in Italy, thousands of flags were shown in the campaign *Pace da tutti i balconi* (“peace from every balcony”) as a protest against the impending war in Iraq. The meaning of “PACE” is thus well-known and the peace flag is used across the world. Sometimes it is replaced with the corresponding translation in the local language.

For the sake of clarity as to the purpose of the formula, the title of this book uses the word “Peace”. In the following chapters, however, the original presentation and explanation of PACE are kept. The formula is registered at the Patent Office in Berlin, Germany, as PACE = B3.i3$^2$.

# Table of Contents

# ACKNOWLEDGMENTS

Without the active support and selfless dedication of hundreds of friends and colleagues from various sites and professional areas in Nepal, this book would not have been possible. Access to information and opportunities for research was made available by them with genuine interest and care. I thank all those concerned for this special chance to live, study and reflect at the heart of Nepali communities. For providing me with the opportunities to interview senior civil servants, members of the security forces and other representatives of the state, as well as to be active in campuses affiliated with the state-owned Tribhuvan University, my thanks go to the Home Office of the Government of Nepal.

Particular acknowledgments in Nepal go to:

Chakra Bahadur Shanker, for introducing me to the Mechi region; the Yogi family in Kathmandu, for providing a heartfelt and supportive base at each visit; the Nembang family in Phidim, for giving me a loving home while I conducted research on site; the Friedrich-Ebert-Stiftung (FES) team, for establishing links with their networks; the campus chiefs and professors at the Phidim campus and at the Taplejung campus, for enabling the program; the headmasters and teachers at the Phidim schools; the dignitaries in both cities, especially DEO Gyan Mani Nepal; the Begha brothers and their families in Chengthapu; Binod Laoti, for broadcasting the program lectures on the community radio; Nanda Nembang and the Alternative Energy Development Centre (AEDC) team, for the provision of a case study; Rosy Chemjong and her family in Phidim; and the Kirat Yakthung Chumlung association, for allowing an in-depth look into the lives of the Limbu people as well as some issues related to the concept of *Limbuwan*.

My closest companion in this venture was my patient assistant, translator and scout, Kulraj Subba, who demonstrated year after year great practical, logistical and psychological skills in assuring success at each step of the project.

ACKNOWLEDGMENTS

My gratitude in Europe goes to:

Silvia da Silva, for her conceptual and statistical support; Guy Warner, for critical reading of the manuscript and taking the PACE formula to new and future levels of application; Michael Strauss, who – as with the first book – edited the work; and Veit Hopf, the publisher, who included this study among his selected works on both peace and South Asian issues, the focus of LIT publishing in Berlin.

# PREFACE

After publishing *Nepal, Zone of Peace* with L'Harmattan in Paris and Bhrikuti Academic Publications in Kathmandu in 2011, my Nepali friends asked me what I would be doing next. They understood my affection for the country and my focus on the nation's *peaceability*. A year before, retired government officer Chakra Bahadur Shanker had kindly taken me to the eastern region. We travelled to the districts of Sunsari and Jhapa in the southeast and then up the hills through Ilam and Panchthar. I wanted to grasp the motives of the people who claimed that the new constitution should recognize eastern districts from north to south as a quasi-autonomous *Limbuwan* province. Nepal, as a single body, was advancing towards post-insurgency socio-political reconciliation under the works of a Ministry of Peace and Reconstruction, with the assistance of a UN Peace Fund and friendly international governments, and thanks to the grassroots actions of civil society and Local Peace Committees in towns and villages.

The harmonization of a post-conflict Nepal, however, was viewed differently by several ethnic groups. Many of the Limbu, Rai, Tamang, Madesh, Tharu, Newari and other peoples saw this time of open debate and power-sharing transition as their chance to establish ethnic-based provinces with accrued autonomy from the center in Kathmandu. Local political power would be linked to their ethnic-based socio-cultural life within renewed historic-geographical boundaries. While welcoming the presence of all other ethnic/caste groups in the provinces as a reflection of cross-regional connections, the definition and meaning of the provincial map could reflect a modern politicization of the ancient symbiosis between place and native populations. This had been a motivating factor for the insurgents during the "People's War" (1996–2006) and a key rallying idea in the Maoists' ideology of the time. I was keen to listen to these people's hopes and fears and to probe their understanding of peace-building in a situation filled with controversies. The eastern region was prone to social unrest with occasional violence in the name of political rights.

In the summer of 2010, during an interaction meeting with local politicians in Ilam, a gentleman suggested I conduct research on peace-building in the context of Nepal's political dissentions and ethnic contentions within the process of constitution-writing. This was relevant indeed. Yet what interested me particularly was how educational establishments were teaching children and young adults the causes and the effects of subsequent systems of repression, rebellion, transition and state-building through consensus. After the launch of *Nepal, Zone of Peace* in Kathmandu (my gratitude goes, among many other people, to Likhat Pandey of Bhrikuti Publications and to Bushan Dahal of Kantipur Television), I decided to observe the measures for peace-building undertaken by teachers, school principals and school management committees, campus lecturers and campus chiefs. The newspapers and national debates were filled with disputes among and within the political parties. Adjacent to this emerged ever larger, visible efforts by civil society, business and educational communities and many other peace-loving groups and individuals who were determined to ensure a violence-free transition phase. What interested me was whether schools and their curriculum acted as a channel through which a peaceable future generation was being instructed by peace-building educators. And, if so, in which way?

In little time, I observed that five years after the Comprehensive Peace Agreement (CPA), most schools were not consciously digesting what had happened to the country in the decade of insurgency, why it had happened, and what lessons may be learned from it. The process of such reflection would need many more years to reach the heart of school life, the teachers' pedagogical approach and the *peace-building agency of the educational establishment and its curriculum*. Understandably, as the enduring trauma was all still very fresh and the many acute points of contention lingered into the peace-building process.

Since observation alone would not suffice for an interesting study (or would have required an extensive longitudinal study across many sites), I proposed to primary and secondary schools in Phidim, in the Panchthar district, and to university campuses in Phidim and Taplejung to allow me to conduct an *action research* in their establishments with occasional interventions over a period of three years. I would give teaching on peace-building for students and teachers, encourage peace-focused education, and observe accordingly if change occurred in understanding, attitude and behavior. My goal was to see if schools could rapidly become "Zones of Peace" when purposely guided in this direction through the concerted efforts of educators (teachers, school managers and parents). Four establishments agreed and gave me access to conduct surveys, give classes and organize interactive programs. The community radio in Phidim broadcast the teaching given on campus and in seminars. A local NGO agreed to become a case study. There were over a hundred interviews and visits of government officers, workshops with community-based organizations and focus groups with politicians. Living at the heart of the community and interacting daily with Nepali change-agents, educationalists, business people and wonderful simple folk for seven weeks each year provided me with experiences and reflections that now make up the backbone of this book.

In May 2011, the Department of Education (Government of Nepal) approved the mandate for all educational establishments to become "Zones of Peace." The directive on "Schools as Zones of Peace" (SZOP) was meant to ensure that schools would be safe havens for children, unharmed by acts of violence. Under this decree, teaching and learning were to take place in an atmosphere free of interference or abuse. In 2012, this directive was again explicitly endorsed with an official meeting in Kathmandu presenting a strategic plan with 14 points to be implemented through the District Education Officers, in cooperation with national civil society and international NGOs such as Save the Children.

SZOP was initially a protective measure to free schools of political influences and secure them as places where physical safety and social tranquility can foster intellectual development and academic improvement. The first idea was that teachers should teach *peacefully*. The second idea – that they should teach *about peace* – was just germinating. This official recognition of Schools as Zones of Peace confirmed my research subject and intensified the mutual understanding between my respondents and me. Interest and willingness deepened over time.

Approaches used for the study are qualitative and quantitative, as well as case-study-based. These combine with a high level of interaction and participation generated from a wide variety of respondents. The action research was a creative space where the people concerned willingly joined in the experiment and applied specific drivers of peace in their profession and immediate environment. It was, in fact, a large project composed of many small projects where the application of peace factors was given in trust in the hands of the respondents who became partners. We hope herewith to make an original contribution to the field of peace education.

This book aims to show the degree to which the SZOP initiative can indeed be translated into meaningful action on the ground. It invites the reader to discuss how teachers, parents and children can embrace peace in their schools and use the SZOP program to redeem and transform – from the bottom up and over time – any pervasive socio-political context of mistrust, tension and rivalries. The next generation needs skills, empowerment, positive examples, visionary and pragmatic thinking, self-esteem, and belief in their country. It is the duty of the previous generation (you and me) to provide healthy grounds for these seeds to grow.

While the study finished in 2014, the publishing could only occur in 2016. This is due to the Great Earthquake of 2015. I was in Kathmandu at the time to do the printing yet put aside this project to join in the emergency relief work. This was, as demonstrated by hundreds of thousands of people, the only right thing to do at the time.

## ABBREVIATIONS

| | |
|---|---|
| ADB | Asian Development Bank |
| AEDC | Alternative Energy Development Center-Nepal |
| bat | Basic trust |
| B3 | Big Three: Social Equity, Good Governance, Sustainable Economic Development |
| CA | Constituent Assembly |
| CBO | Community-based organization |
| CDO | Chief District Officer |
| CPA | Comprehensive Peace Agreement (2006) |
| DCF | District Chief of Forestry |
| emp | Empathy |
| GDP | Gross domestic product |
| GG | Good Governance |
| GPI | Global Peace Index |
| i3 | Individual peace criteria: empathy, locus of control, basic trust |
| loc | Locus of control |
| NPR | Nepali rupee |
| PE | Peace education |
| PCEP | Peace communication educational program |
| SE | Social Equity |
| SED | Social Economic Development |
| SLC | School-Leaving Certificate (after class X) |
| SMC | School Management Committee |
| UNMIN | United Nations (Political) Mission in Nepal (2007–2011) |
| VDC | Village Development Committee |

# INTRODUCTION

## Purpose of the Book

This book aims to contribute to the body of knowledge and practices related to peace education. Teaching the next generations in a peaceful manner and embedding explicit "drivers of peace" throughout national curricula are some of the most sustainable strategies towards the *peaceability* of a country in the long term. The work focuses on Nepal's efforts towards peace education after a period of conflict between insurgents and government. It advocates the placing of peace as a fundamental agent in national designs throughout schools, vocational establishments, universities and informal education, as relevant for all educational systems in the world. All countries could benefit from affirming humanistic tenets, embedding these in teaching plans, structures of establishments, pedagogical skills and attitudes of teachers, as well as explicit expectations placed on inclusive, multicultural bodies of pupils and students. Nepal exemplifies a post-conflict nation that is intently tracing its route towards peace, no matter how difficult it is. The task at hand is to transform national peace efforts into subject matters delivered by teachers and professors that consider themselves as peace-builders.

## Field of Study

The field is the scope and impact of peace education observed in Nepal, and in particular in two schools in Phidim and two campuses affiliated with Tribhuvan University in Kathmandu, one in Phidim and one in Taplejung. It is an *action research* in the tradition of Kurt Lewin whereby the researcher stands in the middle of the experiment, moving from action to observation in a continuous flow of feedback, initiating events and interactions, engaging others to manage change consciously and autonomously, and to share their learning openly.

The research contains observational and experimental components, interventions and surveys that aim to reveal *if*, *when* and *how* "Schools as Zones of Peace" are effective. We seek to highlight the tangible educational peace efforts and dividends that have contributed to preventing a return to armed conflict. Of course, the gradual pacification of the nation after the CPA has not been due to the educational field alone: many expressions of societal engagement and external support have contributed to engendering a state of relative stability despite virulent political disputes. Agents of peace are many in Nepal, both in number and in effectiveness.[1] Our focus here, however, is on the educational field, and in this geographical sampling.

The far eastern, hilly part of the Mechi Zone lent itself well to this action research, with a population composed of Nepali multi-ethnic peoples and Nepali Hindus, and especially with the highest proportion of Limbu people. This region was the scene of violent clashes during the insurgency, and a certain proportion of the Limbu people threatened to secede if their demands for ethno-federalism were ignored by the constitution-makers. Expressions of discontent and conflict have combined to halt social, political and economic development in this area, thus missing opportunities to benefit from some peace dividends. We asked ourselves whether government schools and private establishments were able to maintain a course of peace despite being hindered by this political environment, or whether they succumbed or even subscribed to tendentious education. In particular, we considered:

1. What formula at the individual level may be determinant for maintaining durable peace in society? Which individual characteristics may be correlated to collective peace, and how can these be enhanced through formal and informal education?
2. What educational design, curricula and evaluation methodologies may anchor the educational system as a national pillar of sustainable peacebuilding?

## Hypotheses

This work is based on four hypotheses. The first is that peace education (PE) is a determining contributor to safeguarding social peace during a transition period after a national conflict. The second is that peace in a nation or region is only maintained through a sufficiently large group of single individuals, a critical mass of people who consciously choose peaceful ways despite

---

1 See Duquesne (2011).

conflicting circumstances. It entails the ability of these individuals to create or abide by structures (policies, systems) that are conducive to peace. The third hypothesis is that should fundamental values of Humanity (rights, respect, cooperation, liberty, fulfillment of basic needs) be denied, then even the most peaceful people may turn to violence in the name of peace – as a strategic willed action or in short-lived emotional despair – or else they accept repression or martyrdom. The fourth is that individual peace and collective peace are learnable. For example, the enhancement of an individual characteristic such as *empathy* becomes a collective factor of societal peace expressed as *mutual tolerance*. The reverse effect may be equally true. Embedding these views within a national educational system explicitly would raise the peaceability of a nation – something especially valuable if the nation is walking the long and arduous road of a peace process after acute suffering.

We suggest a peace formula that puts individual and collective peaceability in a relationship of interdependency. This may appear too simplistic to some readers who will argue that a single individual – one who is well-rested, well-fed, personally secure, physically, mentally, emotionally and spiritually sound – may continue to be at peace even in the middle of a conflict. After all, isn't *being at peace no matter the external circumstances* a proof of personal mastery? Yet this can also be the expression of ignorance, self-protection or disregard, which in turn would exacerbate the situation of other people surrounding this individual.

Conflicts affect populations negatively, and only a shared intent for peace by individuals may foster the creation of social circumstances for a peaceful life. We therefore seek to reconcile the power of the individual in maintaining personal peace with the concerted creation of peace-based systems at a collective level.

At the societal level, we identify three characteristics that we shall call the "Big Three" ("B3"): social equity (SE), good governance (GG) and sustainable economic development (SED). Another three characteristics exist at the individual level (the "i3"): empathy (emp), locus of control (loc) and basic trust (bat). The peaceability formula we have created from these is called "PACE." Still in its infancy and being tested in social "laboratories," it still needs to be proven through experiments with various degrees of reversibility of the influential variables.

This book is the outcome of an action research process. Researchers in social and political science are welcome to establish statistical causal links between the PACE formula, B3 and i3. The author welcomes cooperation with professors and students from Nepal's universities to this effect.

## Approach of the Study

The study was observational and experimental. Peace education was introduced to students at the campus of Phidim, Panchthar. Classes towards Bachelor of Education (BEd) degrees and some Master classes received elements of PE through yearly visits over three years. The curriculum covered the B3 variables (SE, GG and SED), peace and conflict theories, practical exercises, case studies, the agency of each person in national peaceability and the prominent role of the teacher in peace-building. These students filled in each year a comprehensive survey on these dimensions. The core of the teaching program was translated and broadcast by radio twice a week during the periods of the experiment. The same survey was also conducted at the same times for a comparable body of students in the campus of Taplejung, the adjacent district. In Taplejung, the students received no interaction regarding peace education, no teaching, and no radio broadcast took place.

Cooperation was formally established with two schools, one "governmental" or "community" school and the other a private school with boarding. Both schools cover primary and secondary levels, from class I to X, for students 6 to 16 years old. While the first school made use of short surveys conducted by the students themselves and received only occasional teaching, the latter was a comprehensive case study with many interactions with the students, training of teachers and the agreement of the principal to implement change to officially declare the school a real Zone of Peace.

To gain a sense of day-to-day social equity, extensive time was spent with the local population and the administrative bodies of the district (town hall, police, health center, water office, chamber of commerce, education office, community-based groups, local Peace Committee office) and a preliminary sampling in the form of a short survey was conducted in 2011 to assess perceptual differences between Limbu and non-Limbu people in the region. This initial sampling, as will be explained later, showed no significant difference between the two population groups.

To approach the dimension of good governance, formal cooperation with a local NGO was made. This NGO teaches GG through training programs across the district. An example of local good governance is the construction of a micro-hydro power plant in the remote village of Siwa, a successful project coordinated by this NGO. We take Siwa as a case study, highlighting the link between SE and GG.

Regarding sustainable economic development, local politicians from 12 different parties were invited to individual interviews and two focus groups that became exploration workshops. Interest and participation was high. The core questions we approached dealt with the role of political parties in the creation of practical programs and concrete systems that link SE, GG and SED for the benefit of the district and eastern region of Nepal.

Finally, two ideas were suggested to two different groups. The first is that the Phidim Municipality become a City of Peace, twinned with another City of Peace in the world. This was suggested to governmental representatives and administrators of the Panchthar district. The second is that the remarkably beautiful upper hills of Chengthapu – deep at the heart of the Limbu historic and cultural region – become the chosen sites for the inception of a peace trail. This trail would serve multiple goals: an attraction for tourists, a means to protect ecological wealth and a site of reverence for ancient and eternal Limbu spirit. This was suggested to the local people and their decision-makers (who are mostly but not only Limbu). The idea was warmly received. It was agreed that its implementation would be fully in line with the concept of a "Zone of Peace," which means that all social, structural and economic systems along the route should be conscious expressions of equity, good governance and sustainable development at the hands of the people who live there.

## Limits to the Study

My presence in Nepal was limited to only seven weeks each year and a very modest self-financed budget. Had there been the possibility to live on-site during the whole of the three years, a different outcome would be available today. Much appreciation goes to the partners in Phidim who remained loyal to the project while I was back in Europe and continued to communicate the values and the goals to be reached. Despite my intermittent presence and observation, the ground covered was extensive and will hopefully be taken as an incentive for others to build on it.

Another limitation was surely the language (spoken words and cultural codes). Though my Nepali assistants and translators did a very good job, highly contextual situations full of ambiguous meanings and rich nuances often escaped my Western, English-speaking mind that is culturally imbued with a German belief in detailed scheduling and a French tendency for directive leadership. Still, hearts did meet, often and deeply.

## Contents of the Book

Chapter 1 is an introduction to peaceability and the formula created from the characteristics at the societal and individual levels (B3 and i3).

Chapter 2 opens the discourse of peace education and its specificity to Nepal.

Chapter 3 discusses the three collective dimensions of B3 characteristics. It delivers extracts of the results from the surveys in both campuses, Phidim and Taplejung.

Chapter 4 presents four case studies aiming to highlight the connection between increased individual peaceability and the shift in collective peace that derives from it.

Chapter 5 attempts to understand the socio-political context of the Limbu people, in particular the idea of *Limbuwan.*

Chapter 6 reflects upon the challenges to PE in Nepal.

The Conclusion encourages the transferability of the PACE formula to all post-conflict environments as well as to relatively stable yet imperfect and continuously challenged democracies across the world. It also cautions about the need to adapt PACE to the uniqueness of places and peoples.

# CHAPTER 1

# PEACEABILITY

> *"The sense of justice is continuous with the love of mankind."*
>
> *John Rawls, A Theory of Justice, 1971*

The core idea of this book reposes on the assumption that peace is learnable. It is *something* that can be taught, a cluster of competences that can be transferred, a set of instruments that can be used. In an efficiency-effectiveness framework, peace can be instructed better, skills can be honed more deeply and applications can be optimized continuously. What is required is an explicit Master Plan that puts peace smack in the middle – for example, in a national educational system, in vocational training or in a development program.

In this chapter, we define a basic vocabulary that will be used repeatedly throughout the book. A formula is presented, inviting readers to test it on a day-to-day basis as well as scientifically. The concept behind the formula is simple yet not easy. It is meant as a mnemonic for members of the tutoring professions – and everyone else – to highlight the mirroring effect between individual consciousness and world affairs, accentuating personal responsibility in the creation of peaceful societies.

The formula is also a peace education tool in and of itself, useful in directing one's attention towards the critical and core components of peaceability while also representing a measurement tool by which entities can be evaluated in terms of a Peaceability Index score.

## 1. Definitions at the Collective Level

*Peaceability* implies that peace is a capacity, a capability. It is a mix of knowledge, experience and application. It emphasizes the mutuality between the micro (personal) art of living in peace on a daily basis and the structural (macro) preservation of collective peace via agreed, stable structures. Peaceability at a collective level is observed in families, villages, provinces, nations, regions and in worldwide systems. It differs in size and characteristics according to time and space. For the purpose of the study, three "drivers" or "dimensions" of collective peaceability were selected: social equity (SE), good governance (GG) and sustainable economic development (SED). Throughout the rest of the book these driving components of collective peaceability are henceforth referred to as "the Big Three" or, more simply, as "B3."

## *Social Equity (SE)*

Social equality is an aspiration of humanity, the desire to live together within norms that ensure that all receive the same respect and treatment – in view of the precept that all fundamentally deserve it. Yet every person develops different talents that will enable some to travel while others stay home, to build a large home while others keep to a hut, to double their wealth while others stay with their initial income. Genetic heritage, natural talent, physical condition, circumstances of life and a plethora of other reasons will combine to make each person particular, exposed to unique situations, and with a personalized understanding of self-responsibility for what happens in his or her life – and whether the person wants to (or is able to) change it.

Total social equality is thus quasi-impossible. Yet the aspiration for it – resisting social systems that may cause dictatorship, tolerate slavery, support invasion, ignore genocide, overlook abuse or declare division as unavoidable – has enflamed the imagination of advocates for revolution and evolution alike. On the one hand, equality has to be deeply fathomed by the exercise of intellect (reason) and spirit (inspiration). Religion, philosophy, education, social change and civil actions are among the inner channels to anchor the profound evidence that all human beings are equal – *by principle*. This is the basis of Human Rights as confirmed by the conventions of the United Nations. On the other hand, equality has to be translated into the construction of government, the instruments of decision-making and the exercise of delivering services back to people who have now become co-creating citizens of their own state. Political approaches to maintaining a stable structure, entrepreneurial liberty within a frame of ethical production and fair taxation, and the liberalization of access to wealth within democratically defined ecological and social legitimacy are some of the outer channels that aim at creating equality – *by decree.*

"In a just society, the liberties of equal citizenship are taken as settled: the rights secured by justice are not subject to political bargaining or to the calculus of social interest," according to John Rawls.[2] This liberal base may provide conceptual and practical stability to states and nations. In the discipline of Public Administration, *social equity* is one of three pillars, the other two being *efficiency* (how quickly and easily services are delivered to citizens) and *economy* (no waste or mismanagement leads to better service for all).

We recognize how difficult it is to translate the aspiration-inspiration of social equality into attitudes and behaviors, and how arduous it is to structure human equality through judicially based systems. That is why, although at times the term *social equity* is interchangeable, it is used predominantly in the text of this study. Whereas social equality may be the "software" (deep yearning, archetypal human code), social equity is the "hardware" (applications and interfaces within social systems and instruments of citizenship).

We assume that social equity is learnable, hence doable – albeit in a constant exercise and care of dynamic equilibrium. The assumption goes as far as deducing that when *social equity* is realized to some extent structurally, then *social equality* leaves the realm of ethereal aspiration and enters the daily consciousness of citizens. Hence social equality, in time, may become a transferable competence of civilization (i.e., learnable) whereby differences are no longer divisions. This is the story of evolution and the quest of human societies. It is deeply political and potentially manageable through ethical, maybe spiritual, certainly rational and rights-based technocracy.

## *Good Governance (GG)*

The OECD defines *good governance* through measurable degrees of participation, transparency, accountability, rule of law, effectiveness and equity: it is "the management of government in a manner that is essentially free of abuse and corruption, and with due regard for the rule of law."[3]

2 Rawls (1971).

3 http://stats.oecd.org/glossary/detail.asp?ID=7237

Those engaged in political science, public administration and development management use it as a qualitative and quantitative framework in which to regulate instances and instruments such as policies, reforms and laws. These organs and mechanisms aim to safeguard and develop equitable state services for populations, maintain a high degree of democracy, protect human rights and advance public and private sector cooperation towards sustainable development. Good governance is a shared space among actors such as government ministries, NGOs and the business community that care to also empower groups which may, if not especially taken into consideration, become vulnerable minorities.

This complex view of good governance is simplified through a distinction between *good vertical governance* and *good horizontal governance*. Vertical governance aims to avoid gaps between local schemes and national policies. Horizontal governance seeks to encourage cross-scale learning among institutions, departments and other stakeholders engaged in local and regional governments. Both should work jointly towards integration and mutual benefit.

UNESCO, using an early framework developed by the OECD, has been delivering educational programs on good governance worldwide in relation to the preservation of cultural heritage as well as the upkeep of peace between peoples. Good governance is taught on the basis of eight characteristics:[4]

1. *Participation:* either direct or through intermediate institutions or representatives. What matters is that the most vulnerable groups in society are brought to the decision-making process. This is possible through liberty of association, freedom of expression and organized civil society.
2. *Transparency:* rules and regulations are either discussed openly (direct democracy) or by representatives who will find agreement in committees. Following this, the enforcement of decisions is consequential because the relevant information is made accessible to all concerned.
3. *Effectiveness and efficiency:* institutionalized processes and procedures are capable of producing results for the good of citizens, seeking a dynamic balance between the fulfillment of both universal and particular needs, as well as the allocation or redistribution of available means and

4 http://portal.unesco.org/ci/en/ev.php-URL_ID=5205&URL_DO=DO_TOPIC&URL_SECTION=201.html

resources. This includes the practice of sustainability in the use of environmental resources.

4. *Responsiveness:* all agents engaged in the practice of good governance are required to act through programs and react to events in a timely way.
5. *Accountability:* governmental institutions, public and private enterprises and all stakeholders are held accountable to the general public. Specific stakeholders are accountable for specific processes and outcomes. Accountability depends on the implementation of the rule of law and on agreed measures of transparency.
6. *Consensus orientation:* Good governance recognizes that there are varied opinions, needs and interests in any society. Therefore, mechanisms to achieve equilibrium and mitigation are required to manage a dynamic and continuously evolving consensus. The interest of the whole should be achieved also by responding to the interests of particular individuals and groups, to the degree that it does not jeopardize the rights or achievements of other groups. Furthermore, such equilibrium depends on the cultural, social and historical contexts of a society and cannot be transposed from one country's system into another.
7. *Equity and inclusiveness:* it is important that all groups and sub-groups in a society perceive themselves as belonging to and counting towards its creation and preservation. The feeling of exclusiveness can lead to depression and to violence. Therefore, good governance is about ensuring that no one is sidelined from the center or mainstream of society, especially if they already suffer from some vulnerability.
8. *Rule of law:* a comprehensive legal framework qualifies the rights and duties of citizens. Enforced impartially, the rule of law protects all people from the violation of their rights, referring to their constitution, national laws and international conventions. It relies, therefore, on an independent and impartial judiciary as well as incorruptible national security and police forces.

We take good governance as a pillar for peace at a collective level. In Nepal, we seek to observe whether political leaders and their executive public officials are accountable, acting in alignment with their mandate; whether citizens (individuals and groups) are enabled to contribute towards local policies and practices; and whether civil society is taken as a valued partner by the local administration, engaging together in cooperative development.

Between 2011 and 2015 (April), this was a difficult enterprise due to both ossified systems and highly volatile circumstances. The constitution had not been written despite two elections of a parliamentary assembly mandated to do so. Acrimonious disputes characterized relations among parties, severely hampering the Parliament's ability to fulfill its tasks. There had not been local elections since 1997. Chiefs of districts for all key departments (government, development, education, police – all reporting to the center in the capital) were nominated by instances in Kathmandu, rotating to new districts every two years. Despite this structural centralization and the opaque transition in state-building, administrators in the eastern hills under observation were keen to use the power given to them to apply good governance as an instrument of the national peace process wherever possible.

### *Sustainable Economic Development (SED)*

Economic development can be basically defined as the "process by which an economy is transformed from one whose rate of growth of per capita income is small or negative to one in which a significant self-sustained rate of increase of per capita income is a permanent long-run feature."[5] Development should, however, also show a qualitative as well as a quantitative change in a given society. Michael P. Todaro and Stephen C. Smith integrate dimensions such as governance, gender, equality, environmental resources and microfinance into the discourse. Sustenance, self-esteem (identity, respect, dignity, recognition) and the freedom to choose (one's economic means and expressions) are also given as core values of development.[6]

Measuring economic development, therefore, is based on several indices such as GDP and the Human Development Index, taking into account literacy rates, life expectancy and the entire portfolio of human capital. The development of an economy is also about how easily goods and services can be delivered to fulfill people's needs. However, needs and the pertinence of goods or services to a people's healthy and meaningful life are subject to debate, or preference. It is the task of politics to mitigate these preferences with reason, to guard from extremes and to protect against the erosion of sustainable sources for common sustenance. Individual financial liberty in the midst of plentiful, collective offers (goods, services, learning)

5 Adelman (1961), 1.

6 Todaro and Smith (2009), 20–22.

with regulatory mechanisms that prohibit greed and redistribute profits equitably could be as close as successful economic development. This stage may well have been achieved at different times in the history of mankind. In any case, economies that rely on the contributions of, and the rewards back to, a small elite only, failing to improve the standard of living of all citizens, cannot be called developed, and certainly not sustainable. Sooner or later, they implode with fratricidal disputes or explode at the hands of insurgents or invaders.

Today, with our planet likened to a global village, the economic development of one country or region has a direct impact on all others and vice versa. Economists at the service of a government seek to juggle differences so as to make an aggregate profit between exports and imports, negotiations of exchange, partnering in industry, buying presence and access to markets, developing production sites and sourcing commodities from near or afar. Relations are intricate and pertain to clear rules (international and commercial law) as well as unspoken, tacit, ones. It is a game of cleverness, but a game that should be equitable. Economic development, to be sustainable, has to be fair, inside the country and among the countries. It is intimately related to good governance and social equity.

The sustainability discourse stresses the ecology of economic activities and the principle by which no development today should endanger the health or survival of future generations. If consuming some goods today implies doubling the amount of efforts in twenty years' time to rid ourselves of the toxic components that helped build the current system, then it is not sustainable. If the opening of resource extraction in a particular region occurs under anonymous control from overseas headquarters that ignore the pollution of coastal land and seashore or the fair economic dividends due back to the local population, then it is not sustainable. If a country is rich in water resources but cannot come up with the national capacity to raise a master-team of civil engineers, surveyors, geologists, technicians, water experts, electricians and managers that will – under a national plan – bring water and electricity to all homes and industries, then this richness does not contribute to improved livelihoods. It may remain deeply ecologically sound if untouched, but it will not channel economic development. There is also an obvious danger of losing control over home water usufruct through the competences and economic superiority of third parties who may impose contracts on resources. Fairness is arbitrary when there is a large difference in power.

Peace, we argue, depends on sustainable economic development. This is not just in the hands of representatives in parliamentary chambers, but in the attitudes and behaviors of a whole nation or communities who are willing to give their best efforts towards common achievement. It is citizens, entrepreneurs, workers, farmers, teachers – indeed, everyone – who must want their economic improvement to be a shared happening and ensure that future generations remain peacefully rich in sustained abundance.

It is feasible to have sustainable and dynamic trade and commercial exchanges, invest in new opportunities that do not harm one another or the planet, engage in healthy business alliances between similar or complementary ventures, and stretch out technological infrastructures and networks for remote communities to link up. These economic visions and goals are positive and should emanate from the populations themselves, not just business schools or universities' economics departments. Economic peace starts when people can pay their bills and have some extra cash for growth. No doubt, an enormous amount of work will make this possible (policies of employment and income distribution, state investment in youth training, boosting of promising sectors, negotiations with trade unions, etc.). This is an effort produced by many muscles. Yet for the motion to make sense and secure enduring motivation, we need a mental model that unites the minds: peace as both the driver and the outcome of sustainable economic development, for example.

## 2. Definitions at the Individual Level

Peaceability at an individual level refers to the psychological capability to regulate one's thoughts and emotions in order to keep an inner state of peace or an equilibrium of contentment despite (or learning from) challenges or suffering. In this view, peace is linked to wisdom, *i.e.*, learning from non-peace to engender more peace. This is a deeply personal journey – no one can do this for another. It is central to the psycho-spiritual growth of each person. Peace is a prerequisite for happiness, which is a mix of profound contentment with what is and gratitude to be a part of it.

Peaceability at the individual level is nonetheless connected to "the other" because it is through feedback that awareness is ignited. Counter-arguments may provide the example of a terrorist who feels inner peace as s/he detonates the bombs on his or her body in a busy marketplace. This being possibly true, then individual peace must be related to the genuine desire that others also enjoy peace, health and wealth.

Opportunities of learning are triggered by others and processed in the inner chambers of the self. Peace learning depends on being attentive to these opportunities, accepting tough lessons at times, and choosing the responses that appear most peaceful. In a cluster of pedagogical (learnable) skills that make up individual peace competence, we have identified three: *Empathy* (emp), *Locus of Control* (loc) and *Basic Trust* (bat). These essential elements of individual peaceability are what we refer to as "i3" throughout the book.

### *Empathy (emp)*

The creators of the Toronto Empathy Questionnaire say that empathy is "a component of social cognition that contributes to one's ability to understand and respond adaptively to others' emotions, succeed in emotional communication, and promote prosocial behavior."[7] This cognitive function refers to the subjective reaction and likely outward action when becoming aware of somebody else's psychological state: if s/he is happy, I share this happiness; if s/he is unhappy, I share and understand this state and offer, if I want to and am able to, my support. Absence of empathy, for example, is when: 1) I am oblivious to the suffering of the other because I cannot relate to it (I see a situation but do not feel what it is like for the other); 2) I am oblivious to it because I don't want to see it and "I don't care" (out of normative habits, self-protection maybe, or to avoid feeling my own powerlessness in finding a remedy); 3) I am happy when the other is unhappy (maybe due to jealousy, revenge, or the beginning stage of cruelty).

Bill Drayton, initiator of Ashoka, a network of social entrepreneurs worldwide,[8] has included the *empathy* factor as a driver for the social business community. In his address to potential social entrepreneurs and explanation of the criteria for admission and awarding of grants, he gives priority

7 Spreng, McKinnon, Mar and Levine (2009).
8 http://empathy.ashoka.org/about-ashokas-empathy-initiative.

to this attribute. Not only should proposals by businesses that "intend to do good" be clear in their response to social needs and sound in their managerial processes, the founders, teams and workers should demonstrate a high level of genuine *empathy*. Grant money would be given on the basis of the business idea making sense, and also on the basis of the strong desire to respond to social needs through commercial ventures. This shows how individual capacity for empathy enters business, hence economic development, while raising social equity.

Empathy is a component of emotional and social intelligence. One's emotional quotient (EQ), like one's intelligence quotient (IQ), is raised through education and socialization. It is learnable in schools, homes, work places, everywhere. By giving it the importance it deserves through public communications, by staging exposure to empathetic behaviors, increased individual peaceability follows suit.

### *Locus of Control (loc)*

A day after the terrorist attacks of 13 November 2015 in Paris, a person dear to me came to visit and enquire about the well-being of my family in France (I live in Germany). After exchanging affectionate words, she said "it's terrible, but there is nothing we can do." Or maybe she said "there is nothing *I* can do." Here Julian B. Rotter and colleagues would say that my friend is an *external* type of person. This means "powerful others" (*e.g.*, terrorists, governments, fate) are in control of events and she is not, even though they touch her life.

Three days later, Deutsche Welle (DW) ran a feature article on the Dalai Lama's response to the massacre in Paris. When asked "How do you view the terror attacks on Paris?" the Dalai Lama responded:

> The twentieth century was a violent one, and more than 200 million people died due to wars and other conflicts. We now see a spillover of the previous century's bloodshed in this century. If we emphasize more on non-violence and harmony, we can herald a new beginning. Unless we make serious attempts to achieve peace, we will continue to see a replay of the mayhem humanity experienced in the 20th century. [...] Humans have created this problem, and now we are asking God to solve it. It is illogical. God would say, solve it yourself because you created it in the first place. [...] We need a systematic approach to foster humanistic values, of oneness and harmony. If we start doing it now, there is hope that this century will

be different from the previous one. It is in everybody's interest. So let us work for peace within our families and society, and not expect help from God, Buddha or the governments.[9]

In terms of locus of control, the Dalai Lama is *internal*: the power to control events, including the change from horrible to good, lies inside each one of us – and nowhere else. Each individual has the power and possibility, within their chosen scope of action, to contribute to peace. This center of power, while influenced by external conditions, may grow in independence and strength as the person "decides" to be personally responsible for peace, whichever level or range of expression he or she may choose.

Locus of control is a personality variable that reflects whether a person believes himself or herself to be in control, or whether external forces are the source of this control. J.B. Rotter, a social psychologist, studied this variable within the scope of the social learning theory[10] and the control theory.[11] This locus is related to other personality traits and we cannot say that "internal" is positive and "external" is negative. We speak only of a tendency to act based on an *a priori* perception and belief regarding one's control over life events.

Refining these previous studies, Fred Rothbaum, John R. Weisz and Samuel S. Snyder further differentiated two categories: primary and secondary control.[12] Primary control refers to actions a person takes to change the world or to try to adapt the world to him or her. Secondary control is about changing oneself to adapt to external demands. This helps define the locus (source of control) by giving a direction or motivation behind the control.[13]

In terms of peace, we are interested in seeing whether people believe that there can be peace in the world to the degree that they themselves act as peacemakers. Some individuals believe that world peace is unattainable because of the "evil in man" (unchangeable forces) yet will personally ac-

---

9 Deutsche Welle (2015).

10 Rotter (1954).

11 Rotter (1966).

12 Rothbaum, Weisz and Snyder (1982).

13 In industrial psychology – how people behave at work – further research was conducted by Paul E. Spector (1988) and Geneviève Fournier and Chantale Jeanrie (1999) to help understand factors influencing motivation, stress management, performance and success. For further work, see Marsh and Richards (1986, 1987).

tively engage in making their immediate environment as peaceful as possible, believing it is their job to do so and that their action brings results (internal control). Others will not invest much in personal accountability and may generally find others responsible (family members, neighbors, politicians) for the lack of peace in their lives. Another group of people will feel personally responsible for peace at a world level, and both primary and secondary aspects of the locus (adapting the self to the world and adapting the world to the self) are dedicated to an unquestionable drive for peace.

The locus of control has been selected as a variable of peaceability because knowing – at an individual level – that one has the power to change from non-peace to peace is a precondition for learning peace skills and honing them for action. Peace education, therefore, will carry an intrinsic value of self-confidence in achieving peace "out there" as a mirroring effect of an increasingly peaceful self-image. We assume that both are under the control of individuals and that this ability is learnable. We also suggest that it should be made learnable through educational curricula.

### *Basic Trust (bat)*

*Basic trust* refers to trust in life as well as in oneself.[14] It may have a component of timelessness whereby it can extend to before birth and after death – *i.e.*, a view of the universe that is benevolent and will respond with goodness because one is deserving this support, either as unconditionally given or as a guaranteed reward against personal effort. Even if we should meet with challenges, even if we should meet face to face with the Devil himself, at the end, all will be good. Quoting peace singer John Lennon, "and if it is not good, then it is not the end."

Child psychologist Erik Erikson (1902–1994) introduced the concept of basic trust in his 1950 work *Childhood and Society*. A student of Freud, Erikson later developed a theory of psychosocial development that expanded Freud's initial five stages of child development to eight stages. A contrast between two psychological states may help to evaluate whether development is more or less successful at each of the eight stages. The first stage is infancy (0–1 year), and the relevant contrast is trust *vs*. mistrust. Another stage, for example, is preschool (4–6 years), with the contrast as

[14] This is embodied in the German noun *Urvertrauen*, composed of *Ur* (origin) and *Vertrauen* (confidence, trust).

initiative *vs*. guilt. "In infancy, the child's major question is whether its world is supportive and predictable; whereas in preschool, the main question is whether the child is good or bad."[15]

The first year of life, therefore, is crucial in establishing basic trust. This will remain a foundation stone for the edifice of the personality throughout life. As an adult building one's life, the quantity of initial basic trust will determine whether the perception of the universe is centrally a supportive one or if it is imbued with haphazardness (no predictability of attention), carelessness (absence of response to need), even enmity (denial of one's right to an enjoyable existence).

The first year of life will not provide generic explanations as to why people succeed in their plans or have positive attitudes. More psychological components and social learning will combine for this. Yet Erikson's heritage is of great value for peace educators. Should basic trust be lacking in infancy, then education – like therapy – may replace or redress an essential psychological attribute for peace with oneself and the world. Furthermore, the capacity to choose whether to trust or not (a given situation or person) derives from a healthy basis of trust that one will normally be protected from harm.

Trust is not naiveté. The differentiation of whether to trust or not to trust is a capacity to judge, intuitionally and/or rationally, and to stand by one's feelings and arguments. This ability in turn is an element of a larger trustful and optimistic self-confidence and confidence in the world. From this derives the basic assumption that one can navigate through life, building trust on fertile land and choosing constructive actions when on barren or hostile grounds. Basic trust also enables one to see suffering as a passage and not an end, and that trust, over time, may grow and even become institutionalized.

Basic trust initially happens at the heart of the family. Parents or guardians are responsible for this. Selecting basic trust as an individual factor of peaceability also implies that peace education, to have an impact upon children, students and adult learners, at best should occur in concert both at school and at home. Teachers and parents correspondingly need to engage in a "can do" discourse: *Yes, we can do peace, because we trust in ourselves and in the world that this is possible.*

---

[15] Kalat (2011).

## 3. The PACE Formula

Peaceability, for short, has been translated into PACE, which of course means peace. We aim to present a digestible and simple – but not simplistic – formula:

$$B3.i3^2 = (SE + GG + SEQ) \times (emp + loc + bat)^2 = PACE$$

*B3* means the "Big Three" dimensions of collective peaceability: SE (social equity), GG (good governance) and SEQ (sustainable economic development).

*i3* refers to the three individual peace competencies, namely: emp (empathy), loc (locus of control) and bat (basic trust).

$PACE = B3.i3^2$ is to be understood as: individual attributes of emp + loc + bat multiplied by collective attributes of SE + GG + SEQ make up a recipe for peace. The fact that i3 is squared shows the significance of the power of the individual to be able to raise the collective "B" factors.

Applying the PACE formula allows for the calculation of a Peaceability Index as the rating for a given population's ability to find peaceful outcomes to political, social or economic problems. It shows a target group's preparedness for peace. The population group may be a local community, a social group, an entire national population or any other predetermined group of people with identified shared characteristics. The Index, as explained, considers two groups of indicator variables concerned with measuring levels of *collective* peaceability (B3) and *individual* peaceability (i3).

Each indicator variable is evaluated through surveys performed of representative target samples of the population that are designed to quantify the presence or absence of each criterion in the population group under study. The results of the population surveys allow the researcher to assign a value to each variable of 0, 1 or 2 on the following basis:

0 – indicates that on average, the survey reported the level of this variable as being absent or at best at such a low level as to exert no positive impact on the peaceability of the population.

1 – indicates that average reported levels of the variable testify to a positive effect on attitudes to peace, but at a sub-optimal level

2 – indicates levels that are considered favorable for contributing greatly to the overall peaceability of the population group. These levels are not necessarily the maximal levels of the variables, as it is arguable if

any population is ever really able to attain maximal values for any of the chosen indicators.

We have observed that the individual or i3 indicator variables are acute determinants of overall peaceability levels of B3. Hence, these values are squared in the PACE Peaceability Index calculation. The presence or absence of each of the i3 peace competency indicator variables (empathy, locus of control and basic trust) has a significant impact on the peaceability level of an individual and also exerts a positive multiplier effect on those collective dimensions of peaceability that may also be present.

The existence, however, of all individual and collective peaceability variables at values of at least 1 is necessary for any given population to have a Peaceability Index level of 27 or above. The threshold of 27 identifies populations whose existing level of peaceability is such that peace and communication education programs can begin to have significant effects on maintaining and continuing to develop and improve peaceability levels.

At a Peaceability Index level below 27, it is necessary to accompany any peace and communication education program with specific actions aimed also at targeting significant improvements in the necessary indicator areas such that values are at least at 1 for all variables. Whatever the Peaceability Index level, all peace and communication education programs should include actions aimed at improving the values of each collective and individual peaceability variable. When values of one or more of the variables are at 0, however, the Peaceability Index level will be below 27 and in these circumstances it becomes important for any program to set objectives that not only improve the values of variables but fundamentally create the necessary ground conditions for peaceability. At levels below 27, the final objective of the program is therefore highly systemic and the necessary resources and pedagogic methods must reflect this all-encompassing, more ambitious objective.

Let us consider various values for the indicator variables and their influence on the resultant PACE Peaceability Index level:

### *PACE Peaceability Index Level 0*

A population that does not have at least a minimal value (value 1) in at least one of the indicator variables – B3 or i3 – will have a PACE Peaceability Index of 0.

Example: the Peaceability Index level for a population will still be 0 if it experiences high levels of social inequality (SE = 0), its local and central government is characterized by inefficiency and corruption (GG = 0), and if there is little or no sustainable economic development (SED = 0) – *even if the values of individual peaceability (emp, loc and bat) all equal 1.* Although individual peaceability is above minimal requirements, the absence of any positive collective peaceability indicator means that peace communication and peace education will have to be accompanied by programs oriented towards raising values of the B3 indicators in order to see improvements in peaceability.

$$\text{PACE} = (0 + 0 + 0).\ (1 + 1 + 1)^2 = 0 \text{ or } \text{PACE} = (1 + 1 + 0).\ (0 + 0 + 0)^2 = 0$$

Both groups of collective and individual variables have to be at least equal to 1 for a PACE Peaceability Index level to be above zero, because at least some degree of individual and collective peaceability needs to be present for a population to be sufficiently receptive to peace education.

### *PACE Peaceability Index Level 1*

The lowest possible PACE Peaceability Index level above zero is 1. A population that has one collective and one individual indicator value at 1, with all others values at 0, will have a PACE Peaceability Index of 1:

$$\text{PACE} = (0 + 0 + 1).\ (0 + 0 + 1)^2 = 1$$

### *PACE Peaceability Index Levels 2–9*

Values of 1 in two B3 indicator variables and in one i3 indicator variable will give a PACE Index value of 2:

$$\text{PACE} = (0 + 1 + 1).\ (0 + 0 + 1)^2 = 2$$

Alternatively, values of 1 in two i3 indicator variables and in only one B3 indicator variable will give a PACE Index value of 4:

$$\text{PACE} = (0 + 0 + 1).\ (0 + 1 + 1)^2 = 4$$

Here we see the relatively important effect of the i3 variables. Peaceability is greater when individual receptiveness to communications of peace values demonstrates higher i3 levels.

With all three i3 indicator variables at 1, the Index value increases to 9:

$$PACE = (0 + 0 + 1). (1 + 1 + 1)^2 = 9$$

... whereas if all B3 variables are at 1 and only one i3 variable is at 1, the PACE Index value will remain at 3:

$$PACE = (1 + 1 + 1). (0 + 0 + 1)^2 = 3$$

### *PACE Peaceability Index Level 27*

Populations whose indicator variables are all at 1 will see a PACE Peaceability Index Level of 27:

$$PACE = (1 + 1 + 1). (1 + 1 + 1)^2 = 27$$

Such populations are optimally primed to accept and to begin to integrate peace communication educational program (PCEP) interventions. We can say that individually and collectively, peace infrastructure is in place such that the PCEP content can be reinvested directly and practically by the participants (snowball effect) and subsequently by the population at large.

Peace-capability is also such that small investments in terms of educational actions can produce large effects on the ground.

We observe in many Westernized societies a tendency to consider peace and communication education as necessary only for developing countries. The values for the peaceability indicators, however, are rarely always at 2 – the "most favorable" level even in the most developed economies. Can developed nations claim that their level of social equity is at 2, when large wealth disparities exist between the wealthiest and the poorest in many of them? Developed countries with large-scale, long-term unemployment and with significant numbers of people homeless and without minimal health care cannot pretend to have social equity values at near optimal levels. Similarly, with all of the other variables, when examined individually and objectively, it is very often possible to show that levels can be improved: with turnout in national and local legislative elections often under 50%, and with

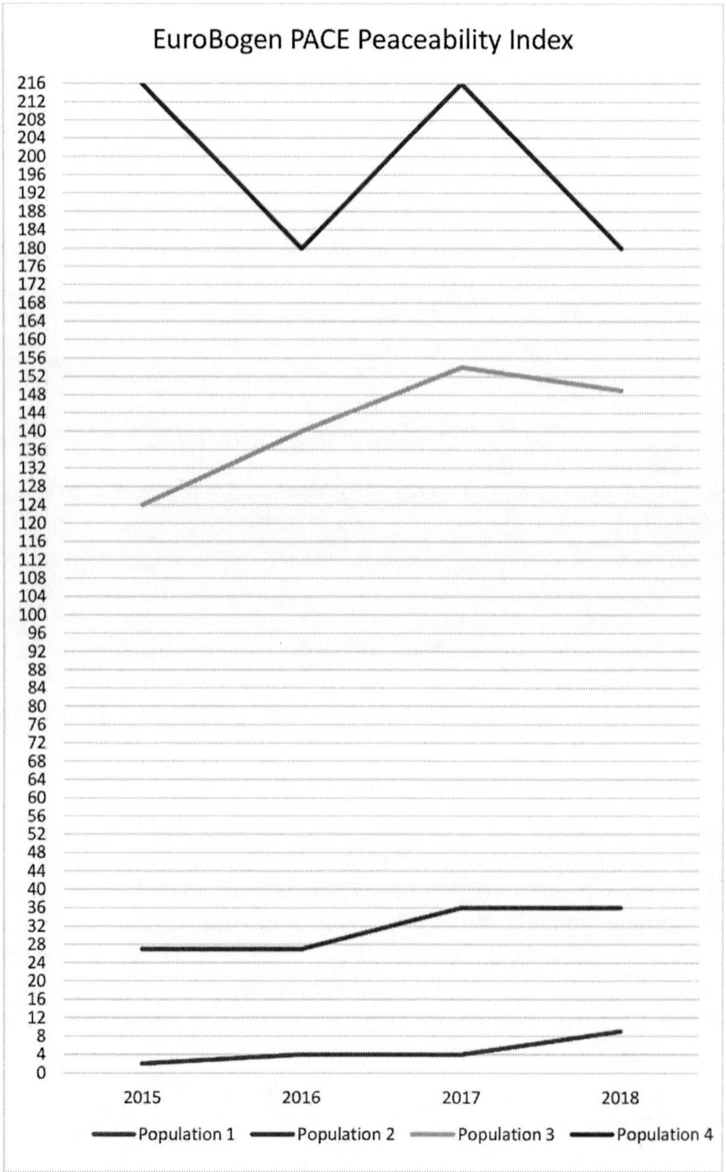
EuroBogen PACE Peaceability Index
216
212
208
204
200
196
192
188
184
180
176
172
168
164
160
156
152
148
144
140
136
132
128
124
120
116
112
108
104
100
96
92
88
84
80
76
72
68
64
60
56
52
48
44
40
36
32
28
24
20
16
12
8
4
0
2015
2016
2017
2018
Population 1
Population 2
Population 3
Population 4

a generalized indifference in politics and government, it becomes more than difficult for many developed nations to attain good governance values of 2. This is just as applicable to the personal locus of control or the communal sustainable development, or indeed for any of the other collective or individual variables.

The formula is meant for each agency everywhere – person or country – at both the *i-level* and the *B-level*. We invite scholars to try it out.

## 4. Relationship to the Global Peace Index

The Institute for Economics and Peace was founded by Australian Stephen Killelea in 2013 to produce, among its other work, a reliable method for calculating a Global Peace Index (GPI). Research teams in Australia, the United States, the United Kingdom and at associated universities support the yearly report on the state of peace according to variables such as the level of safety and security in society, the extent of domestic and international conflict, and the degree of militarization. Like all indices, it is quantitative; it cannot attend to all dimensions or components nor explain the multitude of causal factors behind variances. Nonetheless, it is a pertinent view of the state of the world and is useful to governments and civil society in view of evidence-based policy-making.

The GPI is an extensive list of 23 indicators that are identified and quantified for each country, allowing for a global ranking of national peacefulness. It can be considered as an independent and objective way in which countries, over time, can consider independently or collectively each of the 23 indicators, whilst also tracing the evolution of peacefulness in each country.

Because the PACE Peaceability Index encompasses a different set of measures, it may be used independently of the Global Peace Index or as a complement to it with additional data, specifically from an educational viewpoint, in recognition of where it has limitations.

The GPI identifies indicators for nation states based on primary and secondary data gathered and considered nationally. It does not quantify peacefulness in populations other than at a national scale. Similarly, applying as it does on such a large scale and over such a comprehensive list of indicators, it is not a tool that can be readily applied by experimental researchers on smaller populations. It is by definition an aggregate for each indicator at a national scale to be taken by researchers "as is."

The PACE Peaceability Index is a complementary tool that can be readily applied in the field and at various scales. It is "lighter" in design and in application and is therefore a complementary source of information on levels of local peaceability.

The 23 factors in the GPI range from "instances of violent crime" to "terrorism impact," from "military expenditure" to "deaths from internal conflict," *etc*. All factors, however, are collective and in their nature seem to by-pass the individual's capacity to influence peacefulness at most levels. Of all the indicators, only one, "perceptions of criminality," deals with an individual's personal appreciation of and relationship to the indicator in question.

The PACE Peaceability Index places the individual back at the center of peacefulness and at the heart of the process to improve peaceability. Herein lies a further level of complementarity between the two indices.

The GPI is a measurement tool giving researchers, policy makers and organizations a standardized and longitudinal estimation of peacefulness in each of the countries considered. It is not solution-based in itself, and this can be considered as one of its strengths. Academics, researchers and students from many different disciplines can use and interpret the GPI in considering questions of very different natures, from the effects of militarization to comparable propensities for violent crime. It is a tool that allows for the categorization of a country in terms of its level of peacefulness, which can then inform and guide in a number of directions.

The PACE Peaceability Index, while also being useful in different contexts of research or policy, is directly solution-based and this is its strength. It identifies specifically and measurably the areas for improvement that are needed for peace and where communication and education programs may be optimized.

The GPI relies on data gathered on a national scale and from aggregate data survey sources, analyzed essentially by the Economist Intelligence Unit (EIU) or the Institute for Economics and Peace. In comparison, the data sources for the PACE Peaceability Index are primary sources, garnered through anonymous sample population surveys or small-scale experimental data-collecting. As such, beyond the perfectly reasonable questions of representativeness, what they do allow is a very direct, personal and immediate evaluation of perceptions of peaceability from the individuals or populations partaking in the survey or experiment. Results do not therefore claim to be representative of any population larger than the population directly surveyed. But as far as these individuals are concerned, results are perfectly representative.

When considered together, then, the GPI measure of peacefulness for a national population and a PACE Peaceability Index level for a local population may give excellent aggregates and specific evaluations of preparedness for peace – something particularly useful for peace educators in the field.

One final and important distinction between the two indexes is that the GPI is based around indicators that are negative peace indicators whereas the PACE Peaceability Index focuses on positive peace indicators.

All GPI indicators measure the degree of, or the sum of, non-peaceful acts: prison population, number of homicides, intensity of internal conflict, possession of nuclear and heavy weapons, etc. They implicitly measure the absence of peace without quantifying or qualifying indicators of the presence of peace. The complementarity between the GPI and the PACE Peaceability Index lies in the latter's measurement of positive peace factors. All six of the B3 and i3 indicators measure the presence of variables positively affecting peaceability, rather than the presence of factors negatively affecting peacefulness.

# CHAPTER 2

# PEACE EDUCATION

*Averting war is the work of politicians; establishing peace is the work of education.*

*Maria Montessori*

## 1. Peace Education – Introduction

The PACE formula works under the precept that peace is learnable at individual (i) and collective (B) levels. Peaceability expands with the placing of peace matters within educational programs for children and adults, in formal and informal settings. Peace education has become a field of expertise as a contribution to stabilizing *in-* and *post-*conflict environments in fragile regions. The evidence of systemic and boomerang-like interrelations of all conflicts (between North and South, West and East, rich and poor, psychologies of leaders and militarization, climate change and redistribution of resources…) calls for a universal yet locally adaptable embedding of peace as a central field of knowledge and skills in national and international educational systems.

The latin etymology "e-ducere" refers to drawing out of what is already inherent in a person. Talented educators do so by various means according to the age and circumstances of the learners. A professor providing education to unformed minds will combine input of information, transfer of theoretical and experiential knowledge, and guidance to inquisitive reasoning. Parallel to this, the making of personality, enhancement of character and awakening of responsibility towards the world is a process of kindling psychological matter that is latent, potential, waiting to be called forth. To light a candle in the dark, one has to know that the candle is there and have a box of matches ready for use. If an educator is not convinced that there is a potential bright light inside the learner, then the pedagogy may be technically modern yet remain humanistically dormant. We thus have brilliant engineers who create machines of doom or excellent doctors who try out dangerous drugs on naive populations. Similarly, some religious and political fanatics coming out of the best schools may feel justified to be brutal towards other (and their own) people – in the name of some dictate, power or interest.

Sociological moulds and consequent individual behaviours surely derive from educational backgrounds – styles, formats, purposes. What is taught and how it is taught will leave imprints on the psyche of all recipients and determine much of their actions, generation after generation.

Generally speaking, peace as a subject matter is dealt with in classes on ethics and religion. Correlations to peace are made in history, politics, economics, perhaps geography. There are links to philosophy and psychology. Almost all approaches, however, have a negative driver (*i.e.*, a study of wars or the history of conflicts, or research on the lack of peace and problems deriving from conflict). Whether a subject lesson is connected to peace depends on the personal orientation of the teacher. But it is not (yet) a foundation stone of national curricula, vocational training or adult lifelong education, and this book argues that it should be.

## 2. The United Nations, Grand Master of Peace Education Programs

The largest peace actor is the United Nations (UN). Within the UN system, all agencies, units and funds manage actions aimed at keeping, building or maintaining peace: it is the purpose of the institution to combine social, political, financial and military (blue helmet) forces towards "a world where wars may become obsolete." In areas such as international peace and security, economic and social development, human rights, humanitarian actions, environmental protection or international law, all agencies function as peace educators and peace communicators. Large and adapted educational peace programs are provided in the form of campaigns and curricula.

Many UN-initiated educational peace interventions are conducted through partner organizations such as NGOs or consultancy firms. Together with The Hague Appeal for Peace, for example, in the 2000s, the UN started "peace and small arms education" projects aimed at children and youth in four countries (Albania, Cambodia, Niger and Peru). Engaging teachers and youth, this peace education program (PEP) wanted to reduce violence, increase interest in attending schools and improve academic skills.[16]

UNHCR has an extensive peace education strategy for refugees worldwide.[17] UNESCO has been developing an educational package for 25 years to anchor the precepts and practices of a "peace culture." It conducts both the UNESCO Culture of Peace program[18] and teachers' training to include peace in school curricula. UNICEF has a generic curriculum and works with governments and NGOs to establish schools (and children) as "Zones of Peace," a term used since the 1980s. Close to the UN is the International Network for Education in Emergencies (INEE).[19] This organization, based in Geneva and New York, has a comprehensive package and pedagogical toolkit for teachers freely available. Anyone can learn the basics of peace education in little time by navigating through the available material.[20] This open sharing of pedagogical means towards peace is happening simultaneously across the globe. The German NGO "Ziviler Friedensdienst" (Civil Peace Service) has a teaching compendium for pupils in secondary schools.[21] So do *peaceeducation.org*, *teachforpeace.org* and *educationforpeace.org*, among many others.

Civil society, be it loosely networked or formally organized as NGOs and foundations, is strengthening advocacy campaigns with educational packages for children, youth and adults. Major players in the humanitarian and development fields have their own manuals or are partnering with governments to embed peace lessons in the national curriculum. CARE[22] and Save the Children[23] are but two examples of worldwide organizations embedding peace education in their humanitarian and development programs to continue addressing basic needs and conflict resolution at times of crisis. Governments in post-conflict stages work with the UN and NGOs to implement peace through their educational policies, such as in Sierra Leone, Burundi and Rwanda.[24]

16 United Nations (2004), 133.
17 http://www.unhcr.org/4af7e71d9.html
18 http://www.peace.ca/unesco.htm
19 http://www.ineesite.org/en/
20 http://toolkit.ineesite.org/toolkit/
21 Ziviler Friedensdienst (2010).
22 http://www.care.org/work
23 http://www.savethechildren.org
24 Uwazie (2003).

UPeace, a UN-initiated intergovernmental organization founded in 1980 with university status in Costa Rica, has set an example for other tertiary educational establishments. Bachelor and Master programs in peace studies and peace-related programs are multiplying year-on-year throughout the world, producing thousands of young minds eager to become professional peace-makers. Besides tertiary education, Peace research centers such as PRIO in Oslo or SIPRI in Stockholm, and peace research institutes in Frankfurt, New Delhi, Washington D.C. and many more places are all providing information and tools for furthering peace as a field of study.

Teaching peace is also central to the mission of churches and religiously or morally-oriented philosophies. Buddhism states that individual inner peace is the door to world peace and thus peace teachers will increase their effectiveness only by living peace themselves such as through the practice of compassion.[25] Islam, Christianity, Judaism, Hinduism, Bahai, Quakers, other organized faiths, animistic religions and peace movements of old and modern times have all developed teaching roadmaps to ensure enduring legacies that global peace may be possible one day.[26]

Individual Nobel Peace Prize laureates are recognized for their creation of strategies and operations that have advanced peaceful systems. Peacemakers and peace teachers are, of course, ultimately each and every single human being. In line with the concept of "world citizenship," everyone is a potential peacemaker or peace teacher/communicator. The democratization of peacemaking, the availability of information and the instantaneity of messaging make it possible for peace designs to be implemented in school teaching and extra-curricular activities by any interested formal or informal educator.

This institutional and individual responsibility – to explicitly place peace smack in the middle of curricula from national education, vocational establishments, religious schools and continuous education programs – is a central motive of this book. The UN is no doubt a grand master of peace education projects at the consequential end of conflicts. It is a spender of governments' money for peace programs that may counterbalance some sovereign decisions, themselves at times rather contributing to the upkeep

---

25 Mun (2006), 61.

26 For a comprehensive account of important contributors to significant peace teachings across continents, eras and philosophical traditions, see *Peace Education: Exploring Ethical and Philosophical Foundations*, by James Page (2008).

of fear and violence. A rough caricature of tomorrow's world, should it not choose the path of peace, may be the simple triangulation of weapons traders as economic actors, realist or reactionary governments as political actors and the UN as proxy savior of some trans-continental conscience or the perennial pharmacy for collective wounds.

To ensure that such a pattern does not take hold of humanity's affairs, the governments that willingly spend taxation money for their "cooperation programs" in emerging and developing countries may equally choose to invest in deepening peace education in their homeland. Thus, more individuals would emerge from 10–20 years of education as informed and innovative peacemakers, solution-bringers and healthy personalities to engender a positive step-change in their society and the world community.

## 3. Examples of Peace Education

Thousands of personalities in various fields have developed into peacemakers during or after their professional careers. Millions of individuals, through modest or day-to-day actions, initiate or partake in peacemaking, sometimes unknowingly. Aware of the abundance of educational peace movements and institutions through the centuries and across all cultures, below are three examples chosen from among the many.

### *Maria Montessori and the Montessori Schools*

*The Science of Peace, were it to become a special discipline, would be the most noble of all, for the very life of humanity depends on it. So, also perhaps, does the question of whether our entire civilization evolves or disappears.*

*Dr. Maria Montessori, 1932.*

Based on empirical studies, Maria Montessori[27] developed a systematic process for the development of the child and his or her learning abilities. One key aspect concerns the observance, respect and connection to the child's

[27] Dr. Maria Montessori (1870–1952) was an Italian physician and educator who wrote on scientific pedagogy and introduced a method that continues to grow throughout the world today. Montessori was nominated for the Nobel Peace Prize in 1949, 1950 and 1951. There are Montessori schools in nearly all countries and elements of her method are used in conventional education in public and private schools.

temperament so as to foster his or her self-reliance and access to its own resourcefulness. It is also about self-esteem so that the child feels it can be himself or herself authentically. Individual differences are strengths in the classroom[28] and are leveraged as social prerequisites for tolerance. Another key aspect is the teacher's guidance towards self-regulation by the child in that willful efforts will only be made to the degree that he or she understands the task, its purpose and its social context within the classroom, the family, and later the larger world. Such educational model implicitly teaches peaceability, positioning the ego in a context of social responsibility. The Montessori pedagogy exploits in a practical way the concept of *Locus of Control*, adapting the teaching tools for the development of individual engagement and control over the creation of a "good world," according to the age and uniqueness of the child.

Many Montessori classrooms have a "peace table" where children may go for short periods of silence on their own. It can also be used by the children for conflict resolution through peaceful and respectful communication. Children are encouraged to talk about what is bothering them and how they would wish to find an agreeable solution. Such practice may enter the home environment also.

The Montessori peace pedagogy has extended beyond the classroom setting at crucial times of social conflict. In India, Montessori marches for peace after the inter-religious riots of 1969 in Gujarat State significantly contributed to the restauration of communal harmony. The City Montessori School in Lucknow, India, possibly the largest school in the world with 40,000 pupils, is actively engaged in matters of world peace.[29] Marches are advocacy calls to all world leaders to realize the need for peace by addressing the roots of terrorism and constituting a world parliament to enact comprehensive and binding international laws. This is in accordance with the political teachings and recommendations of many peace-builders, including Mahatma Gandhi.

### *Rudolf Steiner and the Waldorf Schools*

Rudolf Steiner (1861–1925) was an educationalist and social reformer. His writings and teachings proposed a synthesis of science and spirituality,

28 Lloyd (2008).

29 See http://www.cmseducation.org/philosophy.htm

which he sought to express in programs of biodynamic agriculture and a unique style of architecture. He was an *avant-garde* producer of performing arts and founded a cultural center of the arts (The Goetheanum) in Switzerland. In Germany, the first Waldorf Schools (named after the location of the first school) found much resonance, and a movement of Waldorf education gradually spread out to the world. Steiner coined the word "Anthroposophy," a mix of anthropology and philosophy. Anthroposophical medicine uses drugs made of ultra-diluted substances – similar to homeopathy – and accompanies the patient with counselling, meditation and exercises aiming to raise consciousness so as to diagnose the spiritual root cause of the illness and select its holistic remedy.

The education system of a Waldorf school has similarities with the Montessori approach. Waldorf teachers witness the development of the "soul" of each pupil. They teach their lessons in the context of an intelligent world that holds much mystery: mathematics, biology and other subjects help children enter this mystery in order to deduce theories from experience. The teachers' deeper educational function is to escort the forces of good into as much as out of the children's inner life, knowing that light and darkness, good and bad are inherent in everyone. "Meeting one's darkness and having it in rein" is a fundamental self-control or life skill that teachers want to help develop in their pupils, starting from the kindergarten. Waldorf educators are guides in the various development phases of childhood and young adulthood. Besides fostering individual growth, they aim to create a rich social environment in the classroom community. Here the pupils learn social skills, responsibility towards others, *empathy* towards co-students and *understanding* for the world at large.

Later in the higher-secondary and tertiary Waldorf education, the sociological theory of "the Threefold" can be tested in the various disciplines, linking them to each core subject of study. "Social Threefolding" refers to a trilogy of domains – cultural, political and economic. It says that human systems will know dynamic and sustainable health if there is 1) freedom in culture (science, art, religion, education, media); 2) protection of equal rights for all in the political body and the application of laws; and 3) associative cooperation in economic life. Consequently, societies will self-destruct or undergo much suffering if any of these domains controls the others abusively. Religion, for example, should not control politics. Economic interests should not control culture and the media. Politics should not control the free economic development of local communities. The mitigating balance between these three spheres reminds us of the interdependence between Social Equity, Good Governance and Sustainable Economic Development, our collective B3 of the PACE formula.

### *Paulo Freire and Augusto Boal*

Education fosters the process of "conscientization" that helps learners recognize the connections between their individual experiences and the social contexts in which they are embedded. Upon such intellectual "connecting of dots," the *praxis* consists of the engagement of understanding and the application of personal power through action. Brazilian Paulo Freire (1921–1997) followed the logical cycle of theory, application, evaluation, reflection, and then back to theory. A practical sociologist, he said that social transformation is the product of *praxis* at the collective level. Using critical theory, he developed a "Pedagogy of the Oppressed," starting a movement of education that would find significant resonance in Brazil and the South American continent at first (with millions of people then under the oppression of dictatorships) and later across the whole world – in particular in reformist movements.

Public peace education continued outside the classroom, at the heart of the community, with Augusto Boal's (1931–2009) pedagogy of immediate, situational learning. In the Theatre of the Oppressed, students create a theatrical scene – a simulation of conflict or oppression – playing out their roles in positions, postures and verbal expression. Other students – onlookers – enter the scene and play new roles (or the same roles with new behaviors) thus changing the systemic happening. In this way students develop a consciousness for individual roles, personal responsibility, interdependencies of structures and cultures, and the impact of change. The goals are to experience different ways to reach freedom, curb authoritarian and counter-productive tendencies, become aware of others' realities and grow in confidence when taking constructive action. Based on the fact that humans can act and watch themselves as they do so, Boal believed that a human being is a self-contained theatre, actor and spectator in one. Observing ourselves "in action," we can adjust and change these actions to cause different impacts and hence change our world. When he was an administrator in Rio de Janeiro, Boal also created the "legislative theatre" to open a dialogue between citizens and institutional entities and foster a flow of mutual power between them.[30]

Initially grassroots-based and focussing on the poorer communities of South America, both Freire and Boal's pedagogies aim for the learners to "draw out of themselves" (*e-ducere*) that which is needed to create peace. The educationalists left a blueprint for highly effective public awakening, expression of cathartic distress, towards a personal and collective freeing from victimhood. Theatre, debate, dialogue and artistic works reframe socio-economic misfortune into a context of transformation, empowerment and solution-seeking. Education, the practice of freedom and social change become interdependent.

In the context of Freire and Boal's pedagogies and peace-centered experimental research with student groups, it would be feasible to test the PACE formula and the multiplying effect between i3 and B3 variables. Students would define a state of non-peace (causal effects, impacts, structural and cultural manifestations, results in societies and individuals). They would also define a state of peace on similar variables and criteria. Then the theatre would engage in scenarios whereby individuals increase their own *emp*, *loc* and *bat* (each to be determined on a scale of 1–5, for example, with relevant attributes fitting to the scenario).

It would be possible to observe the exponential effect of critical mass (more and more individuals expanding their i3 quotient) upon the structural, cultural and environmental arena, or B3. Like a "period" of reiterating events and exercises over several weeks within a school or university semester, students would experience the interdependence of i3 and B3. In particular, they would observe the development of B3 as a consequence of individual peaceability.

The potency of this causal effect (individual peaceability) could be tested by having two experiments running at the same time with different inputs or different intensity of inputs. For example, responsibility for systems that guarantee *SE, GG and SED* could be entrusted to students

[30] *Legislative theatre*: a process of "transitive democracy" between direct democracy and delegate democracy. Similar to forum theatre in its process, the event is about a proposed law to be passed. Spectators may take the stage and express their opinions, thereby helping with the creation of new, just laws. Several laws were created through legislative theatre during Boal's time in government. The technique then gained recognition in the whole world.

who reach a minimum of 3 in the dimensions of *emp*, *loc* and *bat.* Above 3 would benefit from some teacher's guidance, above 4 would be entirely self-organized. The students themselves would observe and evaluate their results and the reality of PACE. These experiments could happen in summer schools or peace research programs conducting small-n experiments, or be linked across countries via social media with twinning events occurring simultaneously in Iraq, New Zealand, Syria or Finland. The contextual, cross-cultural and pedagogical comparisons would be very valuable to the participants and the entire peace education community.

Peace pedagogy is now a matter of global learning,[31] not just educational injections for temporarily less-peaceful folk. Clearly the cause-and-effect relations are systemic, and of a global nature. Understanding correlations is the task of all populations, whether seemingly peaceful or presently embroiled in conflicts.[32] School teachers, educationalists and university professors are required to become multiplicators of peace pedagogies, anchoring a vision of peace within the social context of the classroom or amphitheatre.[33]

It may be deduced that should peace education fail to enter the educational systems of all nation-states, there is a danger that collective amnesia could erase the memories of previous wars and that new conjurors and propaganda could once again manipulate us to see each other as enemies. Unemployment, overpopulation, economic maldistribution, social discrimination and unchecked personal agendas have many times before combined to incite fear and hatred between otherwise friendly communities.

## 4. Peace Education in Nepal

When the world heard of the violent conflict ignited in 1996 in Nepal, many were baffled: how could the *land of peace* be at war? Imaginations of peaceful villages in the hills and mountains, Buddhist prayers, assiduousness in humble chores, gentle demonstrations of "Namaste" and genuine hospitality everywhere could not be reconciled with fratricide, bombings of precarious small industrial sites or the destruction of schools and health centers

31 Wintersteiner (1999, 2002).
32 Hartmeyer (2008).
33 Hunter (2011).

for Nepalis by Nepalis. It took focused attention to realize that structural violence had been there too deep and too long and that political forces were intent on changing the playing field radically.

Composite views regarding the state of peace today emerge from talking to Nepali people ten years after the CPA. Some deplore the eradication of an "old peace" whereby, despite the archaic and offensive caste system, Nepali people were brothers and sisters who shared simple lives together. Others admit that only a radical shift could have brought Nepal to awake and modernize and that peace would one day be achieved when the leadership and its followers unite their capacity of democracy and good governance.

Of the hundreds of Nepali people who were interviewed and who participated in the study – except for three (a journalist, a teacher and a political scientist) – the all believed that it was abnormal for the Nepali nation to have engaged in a decade of fratricide. They all agreed that everything should be undertaken to make this transition phase as effective as possible in order to reach new shores of peace. They deplored that not enough was done to foster peaceful ways in solving problems and wished they could be more efficient as peacemaking citizens. About half of the people also believed that there were "spoilers," *i.e.*, individuals or small groups who pretend that they want peace but who will cause trouble as soon as peace starts happening (purposely creating a continuous state of crisis). When asked who these people were, answers were vague – sometimes politicians, other times foreigners – but little substantiated or qualified proof was offered.

## *The National Peace Agenda*

When the CPA was signed, the whole nation embarked on a comprehensive peace education agenda. Short- and long-term peace support programs were elaborated and prioritized. Literally all aspects of the country and all segments of society were taken into consideration. How to secure and maintain peace? By addressing the root causes of the conflict and developing peacekeeping and peacemaking capabilities. Transitional justice, law and order, reconstruction, employment schemes, vocational training, economic development, media and public participation towards personal responsibilities in ensuring peace dividends, institutional support for peace, democratic elections, non-partisan political education, ministerial and industrial capacity-building were all among the multiple avenues supported by educational programs.

Civil society, we have seen, is a vibrant segment of the Nepali nation. Personal engagement for the betterment of others' lives is a feature writ large in Nepal. Grassroots movements, small NGOs and CBOs/CSOs, women's groups, associations, clubs and thousands of highly-motivated individuals combine to make a large, flexible and mobile undertaking of peace action. These actors have received, created and disseminated educational programs, teaching combinations of life skills and peaceability. Such organizations travel to rural areas to teach about peace in combination with social, economic and political awareness-raising. Many are funded by the cooperation branches of friendly governments, UN agencies or other IOs.

### *Peace at the Heart of Nepali Pedagogy*

As the national curriculum underwent a large overhaul and new school books were conceived, the "Social Studies" in particular in secondary and higher-secondary levels received a focus on peace, in alignment with the presentation of the international system. The elementary level also was given chapters on "peace in the village." In tertiary education at Tribhuvan University and Kathmandu University, and later also in various other campuses, bachelors and master courses in psychology, sociology, anthropology, political science and other disciplines have been discussing the nature, versatility and plurality of perceptions of peace. The Department of Conflict, Peace and Development Studies of Tribhuvan University, for one, offers both Master and PhD courses in affiliation and partnerships with universities abroad. This program aims to enable students to conduct peace-related research and access employment in institutional and action-related peace professions. The suggestion to create a peace university, similar to the one in Costa Rica, remains an excellent, feasible, and most fitting venture for Nepal.

In its current development and, in view of the resistance to accepting the 2015 constitution by some social groups at the time of writing, schools are still often insecure places with occasional displays of physical violence. Despite efforts in providing training to teachers on child-friendly teaching styles, child psychology, classroom management and the creation of SZOP, the school environment is only slowly revealing itself to the stakeholders (parents, teachers, school managers, students) as a key place where peace starts. The very presentation of knowledge and learning – its purpose and the facilitation towards intellectual, emotional and social intelligence – would benefit from being seen as a foundation for peace.

In the case of Nepal, we see segments of the population that step into the conflict or transition space to spontaneously take on the role of peace educators or mediators. We observe the gradual entry of peace components in the national curriculum and the informal education sector. We also witness support from friendly partners of various sizes and capacities. Yet it is not enough to give Nepal the peace of mind and the self-confidence it needs to transit towards a stable democratic federation and an emerging economy. Peace has to get personal. Peace has to become the rallying point, the main desire in the heart of each citizen. From this shared core motivation, transparent governance and creative economic designs for a small, mostly rural nation can be developed.

Likewise in Europe, in the Americas and on all continents, peace has to enter mainstream schools and institutions as a key driver, whereby peace concepts, practices and skills are disseminated on a much wider scale. Peace is to be recognized as a central nerve in the body of humanity so that we finally realize that when there is no peace in Nepal, Nigeria or Palestine, there can be no peace in France, the UK, Russia or the USA – not real peace now, and certainly not in the long-term. We are all connected and everything matters everywhere.

# CHAPTER 3

# THE COLLECTIVE DIMENSIONS

This chapter gives the essence of a short longitudinal survey that was done over three years, citing samples and extracts that are relevant to the experience of peace. These are supplemented with relevant local information that exemplifies each of the dimensions observed.

Furthermore, a preliminary study involving structured interviews with questionnaires was conducted in 2011. It included a small sample of 10 Limbu families and 10 non-Limbu families representing other castes and ethnicities in Panchthar and Ilam. The questionnaires addressed social, political and economic dimensions. The results revealed a high homogeneity of perceptions and experiences no matter the origin or background of the respondents. Minds seemed to tick "Nepali," and even when defending particular political viewpoints, the comprehensions, motives and argumentations were often very similar. This outcome became an additional incentive for enlarging the body of respondents to approximately one hundred persons (the 2012-2014 survey), and for having a comparison between two sites in two different districts. In those three following years, the study was made with students in Phidim and in Taplejung. All information dates from the period 2011–14.

The selected collective dimensions (the B3 measures) – social equity (SE), good governance (GG) and sustainable economic development (SED) – were each deconstructed into components in order to establish a survey questionnaire. This survey was filled in by students at the public university campus in the town of Phidim (in the district of Panchthar) and by students at the public university campus in the town of Taplejung (in the neighboring northern district of Taplejung). Both campuses are affiliated with the national Tribhuvan University in Kathmandu. The surveys were filled in during one-week periods in the summers of 2012, 2013 and 2014. There were classes, focus groups with local associations, meetings and official public exposures related to peace education in Phidim during one month in each of these years, while in Taplejung only the survey was made without any further peace education program.

Most students were earning bachelors degrees in education (BEd). Some were from other disciplines (commerce, economics, humanities, political science). Some students were at the master's level. For each of the three years, the responding student body was composed of at least 50% of the same people as the year before. In Phidim, the number of respondents was 149 in 2012, 80 in 2013 and 105 in 2014. In Taplejung, there were 135 respondents in 2012, 70 in 2013 and 135 in 2014.

The difference in the number of students completing the questionnaire each year was due to the time of year when the surveys were conducted and to circumstantial events such as holidays, exams planned at short notice, early monsoons and the impossibility for students to reach the campus on foot because of heavy rainfall, or period of strikes that closed the establishments for days. It was difficult to plan a best suitable time in advance while in Europe.

Each year, the respondents spent 2–3 hours filling in a demanding three-part survey in large campus classrooms. The first year – having been assured that students spoke English – the survey was only in English with a teacher's oral translation in the classroom. This proved difficult to manage. By the second year, the survey was in English and Nepali. My appreciation for the students' sustained concentration while filling in the questionnaire runs deep. Likewise for the teachers who assisted.

A final note: while the information from this action research has immediate relevance, the overall study can only be considered complete when two fundamental elements will have been assessed in the longer term: 1) whether students perceived more peace and have contributed to more peace in society over time; and 2) whether our peace program (lectures, radio talks, workshops, focus groups) was instrumental to increased local peace. The latter requires the identification of a causal effect, *i.e.*, provable as being due to the educational activities only or at least partially. Again, campus students would be a perfect population for this continued research. Future researchers may wish to take up on such a challenge or similar task.

## 1. The First Dimension: Social Equity (SE)

The starting point was – and is – "the more *peace education* takes place, the higher the degree of *social equity* in a society." We have seen in the first chapter that social equity is the structural, instrumental balance that enables unavoidable social inequalities to be bearable in a society. In other words, securing equity – *i.e.*, anchoring equality through rights, policies and structures – gives an experience of equality through cultural and societal behaviors, which in turn pacifies a society. Our hypothesis is thus expressed in the following way: *the more peace education, the more social equality; the more social equality, the greater the experience and reality of peace.*

The SE portion of the questionnaire was divided into five parts, each focusing on a set of specific factors:

1. *Social Equality* (six questions): Access to being heard; perceived fairness by all segments of the population in receiving equal quality of public services; access to work opportunities.
2. *Social Equivalency* (eight questions): Access to representation and positions of leadership; enjoyment of fundamental rights; perception of social rights and responsibilities as equally shared; individual capacity to raise the experience of equality in one's local society.
3. *Social Inclusion* (seven questions): Mutual help among Nepali nationals regardless of racial or other classificatory differences; observations of influential factors of discrimination; personal beliefs as to the Nepali nation's ability to unite in spite of, or thanks to, its high social diversity.
4. *Social Capital* (eight questions): Experience related to trust; personal beliefs related to resilience and the attainment of one's goals.
5. *Social Peace* (five questions): Personal actions by the students that directly aim to contribute to increased social peace; perception as to whether there was more social peace than a year earlier.

Two additional questions were asked about general knowledge regarding the Interim Constitution of Nepal and Nepal being a signatory to the International Convention on the Elimination of All Forms of Racial Discrimination. Some questions required a "yes" or "no" answer, while others elicited responses on a scale from 1 (not at all) to 6 (fully). Invisible to the respondents, the questions had a hidden color code reflecting approaches that would later help in assessing the degrees of change in the longitudinal work:

Red = *perception of reality* or *personal experience of reality* (expected change among the students over the three years: the quality of experience).

Yellow = *knowledge* (expected change: increased knowledge regarding peace and instruments of peace development).

Blue = *belief/assumptions/attitude/feelings* (expected change: awareness, empathy, trust and development of internal locus of control).

Green = *propensity of action/concrete peace or non-peace engagement* (expected change: readiness to take personal responsibility).

## *Selected Results: Social Equity*

What follows are selected elements of the results related to the first of the B3, which is SE. The selection is based on statistical significance, whether it may be evidence of a change, a difference between the sites or some other aspect that is relevant to the experience of, or participation in, peace.

*Social Equality,* Question 2 (red, perception/experience): "Police protection is the same for me and my family as for other citizens." Scale: 1 (not true at all) to 6 (very true).

| Equal police protection | 2012 | | 2013 | | 2014 | |
|---|---|---|---|---|---|---|
| | Number of respondents | Average | Number of respondents | Average | Number of respondents | Average |
| Phidim | 96 | 3.4 | 72 | 4.3 | 96 | 3.8 |
| Taplejung | 129 | 3.1 | 48 | 3.8 | 108 | 3.8 |

The data shows the average marks at both sites rising from below the midpoint of 3.5 in 2012 to above it in 2013 and 2014. Overall, we notice a small increase over time, with a large increase from 2012 to 2013 in Phidim and a small drop the following year. In Taplejung, the increase remained stable from 2013 to 2014. We may conclude that the perception of unequal police treatment towards population groups has decreased. This may be due to greater professionalization of the police through training, decreased suspicion over time as the peace process holds, and/or observations that indeed the police are present and helpful for all citizens equally, in principle and in action – in which case an increase of perceived social equality would follow suit.

*Social Equality,* Question 6 (red, perception/experience): "Work opportunities are the same for me and my family as for the other citizens." Scale: 1 (not true at all) to 6 (very true).

| Equal work opportunities | 2012 | | 2013 | | 2014 | |
|---|---|---|---|---|---|---|
| | Number of respondents | Average | Number of respondents | Average | Number of respondents | Average |
| Phidim | 138 | 1.9 | 77 | 2.7 | 102 | 2.7 |
| Taplejung | 132 | 1.5 | 55 | 2.6 | 113 | 2.3 |

We note that at both campuses each year all marks were below 3.5. We also note an increase of values from 2012 to 2014 at each site. In Taplejung, the values are slightly lower than in Phidim. In Taplejung, 44 out of 113 respondents in 2014 gave a mark of 1 (not at all).

In 2012, a qualitative question had followed Question 6, asking: "If no equal access to services or work opportunities, then why not?" Some of the answers were:

"Personal relations and political affiliations get quality of public service."

"Privileges go to own relatives."

"Use of bribes, even force."

"I applied for a post in the army but political parties asked for money, which I did not have. So I am now a student here."

"Political parties hold entrance to jobs."

In 2013 and 2014, in order to shorten the length of the survey, this qualitative question was removed. However, as the quantitative data showed a marked change, it would be interesting to once again probe into people's perceptions and opinions on the equality of access and chances as well as the reasons should these perceptions be maintained.

The difference in the replies to Question 2 (police) and Question 6 (employment) is also of interest. Perceptions of equal treatment by the police were above the midpoint but perceptions of equal work opportunities were below it. There is more confidence in the presence of the police than in one's chances to have personal access to work opportunities. This shows a sign of despair regarding access to employment, which may be due to the fact that people are largely subsistence farmers with little perspective for other type of paid employment. Here we see how the B3s combine, for example social equity (SE) and sustainable economic development (SED).

*Social Equality,* Question 8 (red, perception/experience): "I live in a society where my and my family's fundamental rights (human rights and citizens' rights) are observed and duly protected under the Nepali constitution and the international conventions." To this question, next to a scale of 1 (not at all) to 5 (fully), students had the choice to mark another alternative, which was "I don't know."

| 2012 response scale | Phidim students (149) | Phidim % | Taplejung students (135) | Taplejung % |
|---|---|---|---|---|
| 1 | 37 | 24.8 | 26 | 19.3 |
| 2 | 17 | 11.4 | 25 | 18.5 |
| 3 | 17 | 11.4 | 13 | 9.6 |
| 4 | 18 | 12.1 | 17 | 12.6 |
| 5 | 14 | 9.4 | 18 | 13.3 |
| I don't know | 41 | 27.5 | 35 | 25.9 |
| No answer | 5 | 3.4 | 1 | 0.8 |

| 2013 response scale | Phidim students (79) | Phidim % | Taplejung students (70) | Taplejung % |
|---|---|---|---|---|
| 1 | 8 | 10.1 | 9 | 12.9 |
| 2 | 11 | 13.9 | 7 | 10.0 |
| 3 | 12 | 15.2 | 13 | 18.6 |
| 4 | 5 | 6.3 | 7 | 10.0 |
| 5 | 9 | 11.4 | 5 | 7.1 |
| I don't know | 28 | 35.4 | 12 | 17.1 |
| No answer | 6 | 7.6 | 17 | 24.3 |

| 2014 response scale | Phidim students (107) | Phidim % | Taplejung students (135) | Taplejung % |
|---|---|---|---|---|
| 1 | 10 | 9.3 | 13 | 9.6 |
| 2 | 15 | 14.0 | 20 | 14.8 |
| 3 | 17 | 15.9 | 32 | 23.7 |
| 4 | 36 | 33.6 | 25 | 18.5 |
| 5 | 6 | 5.6 | 9 | 6.7 |
| I don't know | 14 | 13.1 | 12 | 8.9 |
| No answer | 9 | 8.4 | 24 | 17.8 |

What is noticeable in 2012 is the high number of students who chose "I don't know." We take this selection as valid since respondents could otherwise have marked a number or not answered at all. Therefore, an analysis of "not knowing" is required. It seems that although the insurgency based its motives largely on historical redress in the name of people's rights, an actual comprehension of what this practically means in daily life was vague. Fundamental rights are indeed central to (each version of) the Nepali constitution and it is primarily customs and cultural habits that have denied rights tacitly. If a strong instrument to ensure rights is without decentralized implementing measures via good governance or balanced social mechanisms, then the meaning of these principles will elude the population. As for "international conventions," the answers showed that there was almost no awareness about the global body of fundamental human rights.

By 2014, we notice a change: the percentage of "I don't know" has decreased. This may be due to the fact that it was the third year of the action research. By then, many students had been exposed to discourses on rights through our program and also by informal education throughout the country, while access to television and broadcasts of political discussions would have made the notion and the practice of rights more familiar. The longer the peace process has continued, the more teachers have been able to include these topics in their classes. The decrease in "I don't know" responses was accompanied in Taplejung by an increase in the frequency of marks 3 and 4.

*Social equivalency,* Question 9 (yellow, knowledge): "Equality refers to equal rights and equal duties. Some civic duties are enforceable, such as obeying the law, and some are part of the social contract, such as voting. I know my civic duties as a Nepali citizen." Scale: 1 (not at all) to 5 (very well), with an alternative for "I don't know." We present here the results from 2014.

| 2014 response scale | Phidim (107 respondents) | Taplejung (135 respondents) |
|---|---|---|
| 1 | 1 | 2 |
| 2 | 9 | 12 |
| 3 | 28 | 35 |
| 4 | 38 | 30 |
| 5 | 22 | 26 |
| I don't know | 5 | 2 |
| No answer | 4 | 28 |

A high percentage of respondents gave marks 3, 4 and 5. In Taplejung, however, the 28 students who gave no answer, added to the two who said "I don't know," suggest that 22% of the students surveyed still may not think they know their civic duties. This number remains consistently high over the 3 year survey period (26% in 2012, 29% in 2013). Knowledge of civic duties and knowledge about rights go hand-in-hand and are important for the preservation of social peace. At an individual level, the locus of control grows when civic rights and duties are assimilated (through knowledge, acceptance and demonstration) by single citizens, which helps to make the basis of social capital and provides social resilience when consensus-building is necessary at times of disagreement.

*Social Inclusion*. On the topic of "discrimination," the questionnaire had two items relative to a series of traits that may cause discrimination or bias. The first, Question 15, sought responses to the statement "I observe discrimination against people in my society because of *gender*, *race*, *age*, *economic status*, *religion*. The second, Question 16, asked "How often (never, rarely, sometimes, often, always) do I experience discrimination against me because of my*gender*, *race*, *age*, *economic status*, *religion*?"

The data showed that students were more sensitive to observing discrimination towards others than to their personal experience of being discriminated against. In other words, the marks were higher when judging discrimination "out there" than when judging one's own experience of being discriminated against. This trend confirmed itself throughout the three years at both sites.

An analysis of this result may point to some measure of "fantasy" regarding discrimination or injustice compared to actual facts. Psychologically speaking, one "projects" the experience of discrimination onto others even though it does not resonate with one's personal experience. This may be due to the ubiquity of the topic and the in-depth national discussion of the last decades on this crucial subject. Still, individuals may be failing to observe real positive changes that have taken place incrementally in the last years, thanks to the awareness-raising and social peace work provided throughout the region. It could also be a generational gap phenomenon whereby the students belong to a generation that already feels freed from old discriminatory practices while their elder family members and neighbors remain in high perceptions of discrimination due to previous, deeply-embedded, unjust social structures..

*Social Capital,* Question 22 (red, perception/experience): Trust was presented as "being sure of other people's good intentions and knowing that this will last," and the question asked for responses to the statement "Most of the time, I can be sure that other people want the best for me" on a scale of 1 (not at all) to 6 (very true). The results from Phidim were consistently 3.9 each year, while in Taplejung there was an increase from 3.07 in 2012 to 3.44 in 2014.

*Social Capital,* Question 26 (red, perception/experience) asked for responses to the statement "If my life is not going the way I want it, it is other people's fault," using a scale of 1 (not true at all) to 6 (absolutely true). The results from 2014 are shown here.

| 2014 response scale | Phidim (99 respondents) | Taplejung (110 respondents) |
|---|---|---|
| 1 | 49 | 59 |
| 2 | 18 | 22 |
| 3 | 7 | 12 |
| 4 | 5 | 5 |
| 5 | 6 | 5 |
| 6 | 14 | 7 |

We may conclude from this that nearly half of the students in Phidim and over half of the students in Taplejung told themselves that if their life is not going the way they want, there is no gain or justification in blaming this on other people. This is in line with the notion of internal locus of control (loc) whereby individuals see themselves as responsible for the making of, and the results in, their lives. The remaining students felt that the quality of their lives is also the product and the consequences of their socio-political environment, which is influenced by external circumstances such as the work of previous generations or the decisions of current holders of power. To raise the SE factor in a peace-oriented society, we would aim at an even higher percentage of respondents giving a mark of 1 and a similarly large decrease in the number who give 6 – reflecting a less polarized general perception of one's ability to take control of and positively influence one's life outcomes. This is realistically feasible when an environment encourages self-responsibility and accountability as a fundamental personal attribute and as an ingredient for development.

*Social Peace,* Question 32 (red, perception/experience): In responses to the statement "I experience more social peace than one year ago," we see that at both sites there was a continuous overall result near or above the midpoint. The scale went from 1 (not at all) to 6 (very much so) with an option for "I don't know." The latter was agglomerated with the very few absences of answers. We notice that the results are spread out and polarized, with a slight tendency towards 4, 5 and 6 in Phidim and towards 3 and 4 in Taplejung. The increase of respondents marking 6 from 2013 to 2014 is noticeable at both sites.

The question "Is there more social peace than one year ago?" was asked during other meetings, interviews and focus groups, and in all of these circumstances the overwhelming responses during each of the three years of study and in the preliminary work of 2011 were nearly always a clear "yes."

| More peace than one year ago | Phidim 2013 % | Phidim 2013 average mark | Phidim 2014 % | Phidim 2014 average mark |
|---|---|---|---|---|
| 1 | 11.4 | | 3.7 | |
| 2 | 15.2 | | 13.1 | |
| 3 | 11.4 | | 11.2 | |
| 4 | 17.7 | 3.8 | 15.0 | 4.3 |
| 5 | 17.7 | | 20.6 | |
| 6 | 17.7 | | 25.2 | |
| I don't know + n/a | 8.9 | | 11.2 | |

| More peace than one year ago | Taplejung 2013 % | Taplejung 2013 average mark | Taplejung 2014 % | Taplejung 2014 average mark |
|---|---|---|---|---|
| 1 | 11.4 | | 6.7 | |
| 2 | 17.1 | | 13.3 | |
| 3 | 15.7 | | 16.3 | |
| 4 | 18.6 | 3.2 | 12.6 | 3.9 |
| 5 | 8.6 | | 12.6 | |
| 6 | 5.7 | | 20.0 | |
| I don't know + n/a | 22.9 | | 18.5 | |

### *Synopsis of SE Questionnaire Results*

Students found the survey demanding, not only because of its length or the English translation but also due to the content. It asked them to reflect and gauge the accuracy of their judgments. Nearly all of them had never done a survey before and none of them of such nature and length. Still, they gave their full concentration and were keen to be truthful. And since it was all right to answer "I don't know," some pressure was alleviated.

Generally speaking, there were lower marks or more cautious answers in Taplejung than in Phidim, maybe because life is harder in the more remote, colder and mountainous area. The gaps between the two sites were clearer in 2012 than in 2014 – as if a "catching-up" was happening. Students generally expressed their lack of trust towards, or lack of support from, the people in power. They felt sad when looking at their own ambiguity towards their country: besides a deep love for Nepal, there was little hope in becoming capable of making the land flourish. Many students said they wanted at least a bachelor's degree before going to work abroad.

The insurgency and a decade of a fragile peace process had made the young adults of our sample population an awakened but not yet empowered youth. Instruments of development and implementation were still missing. Whenever our peace education suggested that participants should themselves create these instruments, there was not only a feeling of doubt but also clearly an expression of "we don't know how to."

Resilience, a hailed strength of Nepali character, should not be confused with resignation. Karna Sakya made a pertinent plea for entrepreneurial spirit and action in his book *All the Best*,[34] also differentiating one from the other. Nepali resilience is well-demonstrated by the hundreds of thousands of citizens intent on not letting their country fall back into violence even when doubly challenged by earthquakes and political crises. Resignation would be when the powers of nature and the powers-that-be together manage to remove any sense of courage and strength to build or rebuild upon a foundation of self-esteem and inter-community support.

---

[34] Sakya (2014).

## *The Police and Social Peace in Panchthar*

The question regarding whether police protection was the same for every citizen no matter their background was pegged against the data given by the police for the same period. To this effect, there were lengthy qualitative interviews of successive Deputy Superintendents of Police (DSP) and a collecting of data at the police station – three in Phidim and one in Taplejung – during the study period. We shall keep in mind that Panchthar is a rural, remote district with (then) 41 village development committees (VDCs), countless hamlets and stand-alone households. Apart from the "northern highway" starting in Jhapa, crossing Ilam, Phidim and ending in Taplejung, there was little lateral connectivity. The police had to attend to remnant violence and rogue behavior immediately after the signing of the CPA. Six years later, extortion and random intimidation had decreased sharply. Consumption of alcohol was on the increase, especially among the jobless youth. A more "commercial" motive for disputes was on the rise, such as transport companies fighting for customers. When staffed and led by members of opposing political parties, their rivalries would often play out like gang fights at night.

In 2012, quantitative and qualitative data from the police revealed that "crime is on the increase." The DSP explained this with the fact that "Nepal is in a transitional and chaotic phase."[35] The senior officer said that "There is social crime (against women and children), domestic crime, neighborhood crime (hatred) and instant aggression." Agreements concerning good social behaviour had not reached "all the parties' committees in all 41 VDCs. Only 14 VDCs had been reached concerning the legal application of absolute relinquishing of violence related to political divergence."

Then DSP deplored that there was "no stable government, no motivation to defend a rule of law that is neither final nor truly representative, and that no leadership was significantly unifying the public servants or the citizens."

In 2009–10,[36] the police station had registered 62 crimes in Panchthar.

---

35 The interview, data-gathering and interpreting were done in 2012 via translation, as no one at the Phidim Police spoke English.

36 The Nepali calendar is different from the Gregorian one. Since the new year starts in April, a one-year period of data or financial information overlaps two Gregorian calendar years. Data collected from the police corresponds as follows: Nepali years 2065–66 (Gregorian years 2009–10); 2066–67 (2010–11); 2067–68 (2011–12); 2068–69 (2012–

Of these, 22 were heinous crimes (8 involved the use of weapons and one was related to drugs), and there were 40 suicides or deaths by accident.[37] In other words, there was no petty crime or theft reported. Polygamy, crimes against the nation, home violence, incest, extortion and other categories of crime started to be recorded again after the CPA.

In 2010–11, 89 crimes were reported, of which 26 were henious crimes (2 with weapons) and 18 were suicides (5 by poison and 12 by hanging). Five crimes with weapons (three home-made and two ready-made weapons bought on the market) were recorded. The DSP said he observed no presence of international mafia in the hills of Panchthar, and no organized crime such as drug cartels. Generally speaking, there was no noticeable tendency regarding increased possession of weapons. There was one reported instance of human trafficking. The officer said the Phidim prison was initially built for 30 people but contained 80 at the time, some being convicts and others waiting for court judgments.

The Deputy Superintendent was keen to continue working with NGOs and contribute to the dissemination of information about the law, civic behavior and citizen protection. He said that together, the police and the NGOs had been conducting awareness programs throughout the district. Communication with the population was a module in the police training given to all officers in Biratnagar, the minimum being one week of training each year, with more according to job specifications. He identified alcohol as the greatest challenge to social peace, and favored the idea of a law prohibiting alcohol consumption by people under the age of 25. In Panchthar, he said, 90% of people take alcohol, and he regretted that it is available everywhere so cheaply. The making of alcohol at home is also traditional in the district.

Alcohol is consumed for cultural and religious purposes. "In the past, a previous government tried to stop such overwhelming use of alcohol and

13); and 2069–70 (2013–14, the latter year being incomplete at the time of the data collection).

37 It was a surprise at first to see that suicides were considered crimes. While in Europe a suicide would appear in health data (psychological disorder), it is categorized as a crime in Nepal. In other words, to the researcher's eyes, there were only 22 reported "real" crimes in one year in Panchthar. This may be low because social behavior is generally non violent or because crimes are not reported due to social taboos (one does not file complaints about family members, neighbors or friends to the police). Alternatively, there could also be under-reporting because crimes are punished (and reparation exacted) directly by the family or community. This is difficult to establish.

unauthorized wine-selling. They were radical and broke down distilleries. Some social change did take place afterwards but now there are no rules, so crime is increasing as people are again under the influence of alcohol and do things they should not," according to the DSP, who urged that legal controls on alcohol-making and consumption be reinstated.

The causes of crime, said the Deputy Superintendent, were many. They included: 1) poverty, *i.e.*, a consciousness and the reality of insufficiency and unmet needs; 2) revenge, not only related to the past insurgency but also simple disputes that are not mediated or remain without closure; 3) copying international events or trends whereby it has become fashionable to misbehave, as in videos on the Internet or in television series; and 4) heroism, or a sense of heightened ego, if one is defending some idea or some right by *having to* use violence despite one's preference for peace.

Killing is often done by kukuri[38] and pistols, more often under the effect of alcohol than rationally planned. One case had just been filed by a husband who reported that his wife and children had been taken to another country by human traffickers. "Investigation is on-going," said the DSP, "and we remain unsure today whether this information is true or not."

Compared with one year earlier, the DSP could not say if there was more social peace or not. However, he did add that there was definitely more social peace than five years earlier.

The interview concluded on a question related to social inclusion and fairness of protection. The DSP said that the public service ran 24/7. "Despite our availability and well-meaning, some people do not feel that the police is doing a good job because they disagree with the decisions or judgments given at the end of their case. By and large, however, the population is happy with the police because when they call us, we come and help." The officer agreed that civic education and the components of social peace must be taught in schools, and that the media also should communicate about instruments of peace to the mass public. "The villagers must hear this message of peace again and again, and pass it on to their children, in all social groups and at grassroots level."

By 2013, the Deputy Superintendent of Police in Panchthar had changed. The new officer spoke perfect English and welcomed me in

38 The kukuri is the typical curved knife of Nepal that is used for working in the forest. It is also part of the uniform of Nepali Gurkha soldiers.

French. This interview revealed that the Panchthar police force had a planned staff of 450 but only 350 were actually deployed. There were about 100 staff in and around the Phidim headquarters and 250 organized in 33 units to cover the 41 VDCs. The DSP said he lacked manpower (each station has 2 or 3 VDCs, which is "too thin"). Out of these 350 officers, 10% are on regular leave, so in fact only about 300 police men and women were available at any one time. "Beside personnel shortage, we also have logistical constraints. We have only three vehicles for the entire district (two 4x4 pickup trucks and one mini-truck that can carry 20 staff). We do not have enough budget for vehicle maintenance either. There are 93 km to cover from north to south with one reasonable road. All the other roads are in bad conditions or under construction. So it takes us at least two hours to get anywhere! If there is an emergency and we must get somewhere quickly, it is thanks only to our good relations with the locals that motorbikes can be borrowed to reach there more quickly."

This DSP gave a wide-angle, managerial view pointing to the discrepancy between policing as a constitutional obligation and the shortage of logistical support throughout the service to be rendered. He did not blame any one person nor parliamentary politics for this. The government, he said, and even the local population had donated land to build (and rebuild) police stations and police housing. "The police are an element of good governance on behalf of the state. We just have too little means. The Peace Fund has also built new stations with child-friendly and female-friendly environments for our female officers."

Searching for causes of social problems, the DSP confirmed the opinion of his predecessor: petty crime and alcohol are integrated into the lifestyle. If requested to stop drinking, people will refuse because they claim that they cannot quit and argue that "If I don't drink, I cannot work. I won't have the stamina." Many violence-related issues or petty issues are related to alcohol – drunk people get angry and reach for their kukuris; they chop without thinking and the next day, when sober, they regret it. Women can also be perpetrators of domestic violence, because they too drink.

Other problems are socioeconomic in nature: married men are going out of the country to earn wages but do not return. Women, in need of affection, have illicit sexual relationships. In villages, these are regular happenings and at least once a month the police are called to help end the resulting disputes. Family fights can get very violent, even with the killing of babies from illicit relationships.

Another problem is that migrant workers send money from abroad but their spouse misuses it; the migrants are left penniless while abroad, and upon their return they may have no means for themselves. Recently, a woman whose husband was abroad had an affair with a local man. An aunt found out and reprimanded what was happening. The illicit couple planned to kill the aunt. The DSP said the police observe that this sort of situation is on the increase.

Political issues also create problems. Everyone is involved in politics. It has infiltrated all grassroots levels. Teachers, students, transport drivers, tradespeople and everyone else are in some kind of union and they live out the conflict between ideologies in their daily communications with one another. At the district and local levels, politicized citizens will try to alter investigations and decisions made by the police and the courts. Even the police force is politicized, which often leads to stalemates and indecision. The delivery of justice is severely affected by this.

Some situations that turn tragic can even seem ridiculous to some. Several weeks before the interview with this DSP, a 17-year old boy had climbed up an electric pole to impress his girlfriend. As he hung on the wire, he was electrocuted and his body was stuck up there. The locals, with a politicized mind, blamed the electric company for not putting up a board warning against climbing electric poles. For compensation, they asked 50 lakhs for the family. These are the sort of real, day-to-day issues the police deal with.

"Much of the non-peace in Nepal is caused by the political parties at central level," the DSP said (at the time, 33 parties had candidates running in upcoming elections). Some parties caused local disturbances, including physical violence or trying to stop people from getting their citizen registration cards for voting. The people themselves turned against these disturbers. "If the police had not intervened, people would have killed the disturbers, because they were very angry at such action."

The DSP said that "In order to have more social peace, there should be less pressure from political and social group leaders. There should be respect for the rule of law, by all and for all. It is tough; sometimes the police are offered bribes and some officers give in – also for the sake of peace. This, however, is on the wane." In 2014, the numbers of prisoners in the district fluctuated between 90 and 120.

"Yes, there should be advocacy against alcohol. The Community Service Centre fluctuates in the effectiveness of its activities in such awareness-raising campaigns and informal education." The DSP said the various representatives of the government at the district level must work together for a coherent and cohesive advocacy, activating discussions regarding social transformation and changes in personal habits, such as not smoking in public places. The NGOs also do relevant work and should strengthen their partnership with the government, working together for social peace.

When asked if there was more peace than a year earlier, the Deputy Superintendent replied: "I think it is the same. Relatively speaking, Nepal remains a low-crime country compared with other South Asian countries. The hills are especially peaceful. The hills have more Buddhism, a tantric culture and shamanism. The climate is cooler, there is natural space, fewer people. It is open. There is a religious relationship with nature. It is similar to the Native Americans with a traditional approach to natural systems, including the human systems. When people hurt one another, it is almost always under the influence of alcohol, when emotions take over and the mind recedes. Otherwise, people of the hills are by and large very peaceful."

Regarding the interface between the police and the Local Peace Committee office in Phidim, the DSP said "They have 2–3 programs a month and we are invited to speak there. But the partnership is not so strong and their (and our common) effectiveness of action could be higher."

The Deputy Superintendents changed during each year of the study, and in 2014 an interview with a third DSP in Phidim yielded similar information to the previous years. The officer confirmed relatively stable crime rates including suicide and their social causes. He too, said that on the whole, the region was peaceful and had not fallen prey to greater violence due to the fragility of the national peace process. Recorded crimes in the district of Panchthar were 89 in 2010–11, 109 in 2011–12, 110 in 2012–13 and 104 in 2013–14.

From external observation, it seems that the interventions performed by the police reflect a society that struggles with the absence of its male young adults and fathers as they go abroad for better jobs. Upon reflection with assistants and colleagues based on our many interviews and focus groups, it appeared at the time that the discrimination or exclusion of segments of the population from police protection was not a reality, nor was the notion that the police would protect one gender more than another, one geographical location more than another or one ethnic family more than another. Although discrimination had been a key motive for the insurgency and a central discourse in the post-insurgency period, little evidence of it as a societal behavioral characteristic could be seen in this limited observation during that time.

What was obvious, however, was that all of the top police positions, as all other government office representations during the three years of the study, had been held exclusively by members of the Brahmin and Chhettri social groups, directly nominated by ministerial procedures in Kathmandu.[39] The upcoming democracy via local elections would, sooner or later, change this. Then we might observe a greater alignment between the survey data regarding "perceived equality of treatment by the police" and the actual egalitarian police statement of work which genuinely seeks to be devoid of bias and free of discriminatory frameworks.

## *Concluding Discussion*

Social equity may be attained through dynamic and continuous efforts to ensure the systemic and mandatory reallocation of resources towards minorities, curbing the tendency of channeling resources towards the more powerful in society. Unless structurally embedded in the accountability of public administration, the revenue-raising capacities and the privileges that derive from them may soon systematically discriminate against disadvantaged populations. As noted by Frederickson, "Social equity, then, [must] include[s] activities designed to enhance the political power and economic well-being of these minorities."[40]

The Standing Panel of Social Equity in Governance (USA) defines social equity as "the fair, just and equitable management of all institutions serving the public directly or by contract; the fair, just and equitable distribution of public services and implementation of public policy; and the

---

39 Nowadays, the recruitment process is adapting inclusive approaches. Many Janjatis, women, Dalits and Madhesi have entered into the government services. It is noticeable how structures are changing lately, on the basis of policies of inclusiveness.

40 Frederickson (2010), 7.

commitment to promote fairness, justice, and equity in the formation of public policy."

"In a just society, the liberties of equal citizenship are taken as settled: the rights secured by justice are not subject to political bargaining or to the calculus of social interest," according to Rawls.[41] In the discipline of public administration, social equity has become one of three pillars, the other two being efficiency (how quickly and easily services are delivered to citizens) and economy (absence of waste leads to better service for all).

Brenman similarly gives four dimensions of social equity: procedural fairness, access, quality and outcomes.[42] Johnson and Svara also approach social equity from four angles: 1) health care (who can afford which care, who gets hospitalization first, who is covered by which insurance); 2) criminal justice (crime levels according to communities, response and case processing times, and recidivism rates); 3) education (who gets which type of education in which establishment to achieve which level); and 4) personnel policies in private and public enterprises (discrimination, equal opportunities, promotion, interview styles).[43]

If we take health care, for example, inequity is when underprivileged segments of the population suffer a lack of health through social factors such as "unhealthy health practices, poverty, unemployment and underemployment, racism and discrimination, housing, transportation and other neighborhood environmental conditions."[44] Social equity would entail the expansion of health agencies to these populations, health training in communities, availability of vehicles to take patients to health centers and local community nurses and doctors that do not privilege particular social groups over others. Financial resource distribution would have to be dedicated to these recipients. A comparison of health services offered to various communities can be, for example, maternal and infant health, or access to dental care. In my meeting with the health authorities in Panchthar in 2013, the Chief of Staff presented the first results from the District Poverty Monitoring and Analysis System. This program, launched in 2011 especially for the remote areas, revealed increased access to health, comparable to the increase of access to education.

---

41 Rawls (1971).

42 Brenman (2010).

43 Johnson and Svara (2011).

44 Lavizzo-Mourey *et al.* (2005), quoted in *ibid.*, 139.

Barbarin and Richter write in their studies on South Africa that "once the celebrations of the democratic election were over, few were surprised to find that the dream of social equality and economic progress for many citizens remained as elusive as ever."[45] Social equality is a key motivator in evolutionary or revolutionary change but cannot happen overnight, especially on the historical foundation of highly segregated or stratified groups. It takes time, and a lot of commitment.

Three main avenues may lead in parallel to the normalization of equality as a notion, at least, and its gradual concretization in a pluralistic society, over years. The first is *access to posts of leadership* by any candidate no matter their race, origin, gender or age on the basis of capability and merit, through fair elections. The second is *education about, protection of and promotion of every individual's fundamental rights*. Taking the perspective of human rights (according to universal conventions) or citizens' rights (according to the constitution) means that people are protected by the rule of law and the institutions of order and justice. The third is the *right to employment*, with equal access to opportunities for work or for creating enterprises. A system that binds employment rights, shared leadership and communal order is that of cooperatives or enterprises that create a structure, culture and decision-making apparatus of co-ownership. This equitable system is adaptable to small and large organizations.

A World Bank document on social exclusion contributing to the EU's Social Inclusion Agenda defines both exclusion and inclusion:

- *Social exclusion* is a process whereby certain individuals are pushed to the edge of society and prevented from participating fully by virtue of their poverty, or lack of basic competencies and lifelong learning opportunities, or as a result of discrimination. This distances them from jobs, income and education, and training opportunities, as well as social and community networks and activities.

  They have little access to power and decision-making bodies, and thus often feel powerless and unable to take control over the decisions that affect their day to day lives.
- *Social inclusion* is a process which ensures that those at risk of poverty and social exclusion gain the opportunities and resources necessary to participate fully in economic, social and cultural life, and to enjoy a stan-

[45] Barbarin and Richter (2001).

dard of living and well-being that is considered normal in the society in which they live. It ensures that they have a greater participation in the decision making which affects their lives and access to their fundamental rights.[46]

Exclusion occurs when social and economic factors prevent individuals in a society from ever reaching their full potential. Deprivation of certain socioeconomic capabilities leads to being barred from participating in the labor force, consuming goods and services, or accumulating wealth. The World Bank study measured four forms of capital:

- *Financial capital:* owning financial assets or having the ability to acquire financial capital through employment earnings, farming, rental and investment income. Financial capital gives the power to participate in exchanges and trade.
- *Physical capital:* privately owning land or property. It also includes neighborhood infrastructure and assets that facilitate access to education and social activities.
- *Human capital:* achieved through education and years of schooling and training. Lacking education capital is defined as not having reached the compulsory level of education in one's country.
- *Social capital:* having access to social networks and relationships that allow individuals to achieve reciprocated goals. Both social equity and social equality merge in the concept of social capital. A society with higher social capital is a society which displays active networks and mutual support, hence contributing to higher quality community governance. This has a positive impact on economic, social and personal development.[47]

Exclusion is therefore attempted to be measured in terms of forms of capital. For a full analysis of exclusion, what matters is not only the relationship between these four forms of capital but also the implicit manner with which structures of power maintain a society in a *status quo*. Non-participation is as much an outcome of power abuse in the social structure as the inability of an individual or a family to stay clear of alcohol or drugs.

We encourage students and social scientists to take this study further and to point to the creation and use of effective instruments for social equity, so that Nepal can enjoy the social peace it deserves.

---

46 World Bank (2007).

47 *Ibid.*

## 2. The Second Dimension: Good Governance (GG)

Our hypothesis states that "the *more peace education* takes place, the *better the governance* of a society." To educate about peace is to teach or facilitate an understanding and an application of societal regulation that protects and develops human dignity in a healthy environment. Good governance refers to the commitment by administrators and governors – who are accountable individually and collectively as commissions, committees, agencies and ministries – to the alignment of processes and procedures with the ultimate deontology they aim to incarnate. Governance may be defined as the systemic and systematic translation of societal order and evolution through dynamic and interactive relations between all stakeholders. Since conflicts of interests cannot be avoided, GG requires structural and organizational talent for regulating conflict, reaching consensus and legislating matters that pertain to social equity. Crucial to this field is *transparency*, which, by principle, keeps corruption or hurtful practices in check.

As explained in Chapter 1, the "governance" we mean is a combination of policies, legislation and implementation systems that provides a fair order for a society, the management of its resources and the redistribution of the fruit of its work as equitably as possible. The context is democratic, whereby citizens, as legal entities whose rights are protected by law, have the power to decide the direction of their nation. This occurs via a system of information, consultation, and voting. The more direct the democracy, the more detailed the information and the more frequent the voting. The more indirect the democracy, the more power resides in the hands of elected representatives who may run the risk of distancing themselves from the voters and making decisions without their participation. This in turn can run counter to peace if the citizens think that their government is not listening to them and is abusing their trust. Social unrest may be a consequence.

In the context of Nepal at the time of writing, GG was still a vague concept, especially in remote places. Teachers had difficulty explaining it to their classes in rural areas. There had not been local elections for two decades, and the language of violence was still used here and there to impose personal views where the rule of law was either absent or discredited.

During teaching sessions at the Phidim campus, we discussed GG and whether the Nepali people would be able to find a way that aligned the legislators in Kathmandu with the reality of the peasants in the hills. The competences required for resource management and economic development seemed daunting to the students who nonetheless felt that, with time, they might possibly one day master such tasks. It was mostly their mistrust in the disputes among party leaders and cadres that cast a shadow on their enthusiasm for GG as a pillar of peace. "We can make good laws" they would say, "but what to do when leaders do not apply them for themselves and their own party?"

This question will be asked to the governments of all countries in the world. Double standards are ubiquitous and the temptation for abuse is not attached to any particular flag. Many legitimized or legalized actions today will be judged by history as having been disgraceful and damaging – as was the case of slavery after the practice had flourished for centuries in many regions. This is why the PACE formula has the individual conscience and personal attitude embedded in it – within the "i" criterion (subdivided into empathy, locus of control and basic trust). By being squared, the "i" emphasizes the importance and weight of each individual taking the collective values at a personal level. In this way, GG may work collectively (bottom-up and laterally) as compared to being a technocratic imposition upon a population (top-down).

In our study, we thus stated that "*the better the governance, the more peace*." Social peace and individual peace within a society also depend upon good governance. It is therefore relevant for national educational systems – as guarantors of peace – to include a didactic presentation of GG and foster an understanding of pupils' and students' personal responsibility to act as advocates for peace through observance and optimization of governance.

The GG portion of the questionnaire[48] was sub-divided into twelve elements:

1. *Attendance* (one question)
2. *Consultation* (five questions)
3. *Good governance* – Politics and Administration (eight questions)

[48] Among the sources for the questionnaire design on GG were the Council of Europe (CoE), Asian Barometer, Afesis-Corplan, Good Governance Learning Network (GGLN), Gesellschaft für Internationale Zusammenarbeit (GIZ), Canadian International Development Agency (CIDA), Organisation for Economic Cooperation and Development (OECD), Mindlab, Economic Commission for Africa (ECA) and Human Resources and Skills Development Canada (HRSDC).

4. *Transparency* (three questions)
5. *Agreement* (two questions)
6. *Disclosure* (two questions)
7. *Reporting on performance* (one question)
8. *Rule of law* (three questions)
9. *Corruption* (two questions)
10. *Conflict regulation and mediation* (eight questions)
11. *Democracy* (four questions)
12. *Political peace* (eleven questions)

### *Selected Results: Good Governance*

*Consultation*, Question 4 (red, perception/experience): "Generally speaking, at public meetings, I (or other members of my family) can express a disagreement without fear of reprisal." Scale: 1 (not at all) to 6 (fully), with the possibility to respond "I don't know."

| Can express disagreement in public meetings without fear of reprisal | Phidim (105 respondents) 2014 % | Taplejung (132 respondents) 2014 % |
|---|---|---|
| 1 | 28.6 | 26.5 |
| 2 | 7.6 | 13.6 |
| 3 | 2.9 | 8.3 |
| 4 | 8.6 | 5.3 |
| 5 | 13.3 | 6.9 |
| 6 | 15.2 | 10.6 |
| I don't know | 12.0 | 14.4 |
| No answer | 11.8 | 14.4 |
| Average | 3.2 | 2.8 |

That 28.6% in Phidim and 26.5% in Taplejung should say that they cannot express disagreement without fear of reprisal is an important statement. The aggregated percentages of scale points 4 to 6, amounting to 37.1% in Phidim and 22.8% in Taplejung, also show polarization and that large numbers of people have diverging perceptions of the same phenomemon. This may be due to very different factors, such as the frustration of not having local elections or an exposure to teachers and professors with different political discourses. The overall average in 2014 was 3.2 in Phidim and 2.8 in

Taplejung. In the previous year, it had been the same in Phidim (3.2) and lower yet comparable in Taplejung (2.6).

If GG were taught at school and in informal training, we may expect a reduction of the scores 1–3 and "I don't know," and an increase in scores 4–6. Not being afraid of reprisal for one's opinion is linked to the experience of trust, which is an element of social capital (also found in the SE portion of the questionnaire).

*Politics and Administration*, Question 9 (blue, beliefs / assumptions / attitudes / feelings): "I believe civil servants are doing the best they can under the circumstances or constraints they experience." Scale: 1 (not at all) to 6 (very much so), with the possibility to respond "I don't know."

| Civil servants are doing their best | Phidim 2012 % | Phidim 2013 % | Phidim 2014 % | Taplejung 2012 % | Taplejung 2013 % | Taplejung 2014 % |
|---|---|---|---|---|---|---|
| 1 | 14.2 | 16.3 | 11.4 | 26.6 | 23.9 | 22.7 |
| 2 | 11.9 | 13.8 | 13.3 | 23.7 | 19.4 | 22.0 |
| 3 | 14.9 | 8.8 | 6.7 | 18.0 | 13.4 | 14.4 |
| 4 | 20.9 | 17.5 | 16.2 | 12.9 | 4.5 | 6.8 |
| 5 | 20.9 | 18.8 | 18.1 | 7.9 | 9.0 | 6.8 |
| 6 | 14.9 | 12.5 | 20.0 | 7.9 | 7.5 | 10.6 |
| I don't know + no answer | 2.2 | 12.5 | 14.3 | 2.9 | 22.4 | 16.6 |
| Average | 3.7 | 3.5 | 3.9 | 2.7 | 2.7 | 2.8 |

This data shows, at both sites over the three years, there was a very slight increase in the belief that *civil servants are doing their best under the circumstance or constraints*, with Phidim at or above the midpoint of 3.5 and Taplejung below the same mark. Even if the increase was small, it may point to an affirmation of the civil servants themselves. When civil servants are recognized personally as individuals striving to do their best, it is a positive sign of confidence in the civil service, itself a part of social capital. Having a pre-existing positive perception of public service agents can be a vector for positive change in good governance practices throughout public administration and civil society.

*Political Engagement,* Questions 10–14 (green, propensity of action/concrete peace engagement) asked whether students had taken part in some particular political activities in the past year. This is the data for 2014 only, with percentages rounded off to the nearest whole number.

| In the last year… | Phidim Yes % | Phidim No % | Taplejung Yes % | Taplejung No % |
|---|---|---|---|---|
| I signed a petition | 20 | 80 | 14 | 86 |
| I searched for unprejudiced political information | 34 | 66 | 25 | 75 |
| I participated in a political debate or dialogue | 38 | 62 | 21 | 79 |
| I participated in a demonstration or march | 44 | 56 | 34 | 66 |
| I used aggression to express frustration in political matters | 12 | 88 | 14 | 86 |

The data shows that there is a higher propensity not to engage in political activities than to engage in them. The causes of this were not studied, but we may assume that some students did not feel well-equipped to have a political opinion they could really defend. We might also assume that political engagement could still be perceived as threatening (fear of reprisal or fear of identifying oneself with one's beliefs): at both sites, the highest-marked political activity was "participation in a demo or march" (44% for Phidim and 34% for Taplejung); maybe this type of activity is the most anonymous. We may also presume a general lack of information, awareness or political education that depreciates enthusiasm for direct, vocal, face-to-face, public and consensus-oriented participation.

*Transparency,* Question 15 (red, perception/experience): "We are informed by our government agencies about the management of public resources (water, land, forest, infrastructure)." Here, average marks increased each year at both sites – at Phidim, from 2.5 in 2012 to 4.4 in 2014; and at Taplejung, from 2.6 to 3.9.

| We are informed about the management of resources | Phidim 2012 | Phidim 2013 | Phidim 2014 | Taplejung 2012 | Taplejung 2013 | Taplejung 2014 |
|---|---|---|---|---|---|---|
| Average mark | 2.5 | 4.3 | 4.4 | 2.6 | 3.7 | 3.9 |

*Agreement,* Question 19 (green, action/concrete engagement) probed the propensity of respondents to taking personal action regarding the management of public resources. The students responded to the following statement: "If I disagree with the management of local resources, I open a constructive debate about it." Scale: 1 (not at all) to 6 (absolutely / regularly), with the possibility to respond "I don't know." The percentages given below are rounded off.

| I open debate about public resource management | Phidim 2012 % | Phidim 2013 % | Phidim 2014 % | Taplejung 2012 % | Taplejung 2013 % | Taplejung 2014 % |
|---|---|---|---|---|---|---|
| 1 | 9 | 20 | 16 | 19 | 18 | 16 |
| 2 | 12 | 5 | 8 | 19 | 8 | 8 |
| 3 | 13 | 6 | 7 | 25 | 15 | 7 |
| 4 | 13 | 7 | 7 | 14 | 10 | 7 |
| 5 | 13 | 19 | 12 | 4 | 7 | 12 |
| 6 | 34 | 34 | 32 | 6 | 18 | 32 |
| I don't know + no answer | 6 | 9 | 18 | 13 | 24 | 18 |
| Average mark | 4.2 | 4.1 | 4.1 | 2.8 | 2.8 | 4.1 |

This data shows a constant propensity for action in Phidim and a large increase for Taplejung in 2014 after two consecutive years of being lower. In view of the fact that Questions 10–14 on political engagement gave the impression that students were not prone to participating in political actions, we must take the results of Question 19 with some degree of caution. Some information to cross-check the propensity of students to engage in governance can be found in their engagement in community-based organizations (CBOs) or non-governmental organizations (NGOs).

*Disclosure,* Question 21 (red, perception/experience): "We are informed about how our local and national taxes are re-invested into the local area for development." Scale: 1 (not at all) to 6 (very well), with the possibility to respond "I don't know."

| Informed on taxes reinvested locally | Phidim 2012 % | Phidim 2013 % | Phidim 2014 % | Taplejung 2012 % | Taplejung 2013 % | Taplejung 2014 % |
|---|---|---|---|---|---|---|
| Respondents | 134<br>-1 n/a | 80<br>-13 n/a | 105<br>-29 n/a | 138<br>-1 n/a | 67<br>-18 n/a | 132<br>-38 n/a |
| 1 | 56.0 | 8.8 | 4.8 | 31.7 | 13.4 | 13.6 |
| 2 | 11.2 | 16.3 | 11.4 | 24.5 | 11.9 | 14.4 |
| 3 | 11.2 | 26.3 | 16.2 | 18.7 | 10.4 | 12.9 |
| 4 | 6.0 | 11.3 | 14.3 | 10.8 | 13.4 | 10.6 |
| 5 | 8.2 | 11.3 | 10.5 | 7.9 | 19.4 | 11.4 |
| 6 | 6.7 | 10.0 | 15.2 | 5.8 | 4.5 | 8.3 |
| I don't know + no answer | 0.7 | 16.3 | 27.6 | 0.7 | 26.9 | 28.8 |
| Average mark | 2.2 | 3.4 | 3.8 | 2.6 | 3.4 | 3.2 |

The percentage results show a decrease in the perception of a total lack of information and an overall increase in the perception that information regarding the use of tax money for local public projects is being disclosed. The pattern is clearer in Phidim than in Taplejung. In view of the polarity in results and the increasing amount of students who either responded "I don't know" or did not respond to this question, the results seem to indicate a lack of data, a lack of principled transparency or a lack of equality in access to information regarding tax expenditures.

*Reporting on Performance,* Question 22 (red, perception/experience): "After our leaders have gained our vote or support, they later report to us on the performance of their actions." This question had a similar scale of 1 (not at all) to 6 (very well), with the option for responding "I don't know." We report here the results of 2014:

| Leaders report on their performance | Phidim 2014 % (105 students - 17 n/a) | Taplejung 2014 % (132 students - 25 n/a) |
|---|---|---|
| 1 | 32.4 | 36.4 |
| 2 | 15.2 | 12.9 |
| 3 | 15.2 | 10.6 |
| 4 | 6.7 | 9.1 |
| 5 | 3.8 | 3.8 |
| 6 | 10.5 | 8.3 |
| I don't know + no answer | 16.2 | 18,9 |
| Average mark from actual respondents | 2.6 | 2.5 |

In both Phidim and Taplejung, more than two-thirds of the students answered with marks lower than 3.5 (the midpoint) or "I don't know." Being unaware of the actual results of what elected politicians have done, or being aware of an absence of reporting on their performance, may lead to interpretations that GG performance is either low or undisclosed. This may be conducive to political dissatisfaction or the possibility for irregularities to go unchecked, which in turn leads to social inequity and non-peace.

*Corruption,* Question 26 (blue, beliefs/assumptions): The statement "I trust my government representatives will not enrich themselves at my expense" had responses on a scale from 1 (not at all) to 6 (trust fully) with the possibility to respond "I don't know." We show here the sample of Phidim in 2014 only, noting that the aggregate of "I don't know" and non-responses consisted mostly of students responding "I don't know."

| I trust my government representatives will not enrich themselves at my expense | Phidim 2014 (105 respondents - 31 n/a) % |
|---|---|
| 1 | 17.1 |
| 2 | 9.5 |
| 3 | 14.3 |
| 4 | 9.5 |
| 5 | 9.5 |
| 6 | 10.5 |
| I don't know + no answer | 29.5 |
| Average mark from those responding 1-6 | 3.2 |

The results of Question 26 seem in alignment with those of Question 22 with average marks around or below 3. This may point to a genuine lack of trust in the "establishment" and its capacity to perform or develop good governance, or it may show that the respondents are generally not informed about the instruments of good governance and thus display a low level of knowledge and experience by selecting "I don't know."

*Conflict Regulation and Mediation,* Question 28 (red, perception/experience): "There is here a local, traditional, informal system for solving conflicts which works for me and my family (e.g., through our elders)." In 2014, the average on the scale of 1 (not at all) to 6 (very much so) was 4.1 for both Phidim and Taplejung.

| There is here a traditional system for solving conflicts which works | Phidim 2014 (105 students – 18 n/a) % | Taplejung 2014 (132 students – 28 n/a) % |
|---|---|---|
| 1 | 7.6 | 8.3 |
| 2 | 9.5 | 8.3 |
| 3 | 13.3 | 11.4 |
| 4 | 10.5 | 16.7 |
| 5 | 16.2 | 9.1 |
| 6 | 25.7 | 25.0 |
| I don't know + no answer | 17.1 | 21.2 |
| Average mark | 4.1 | 4.1 |

This result may be interpreted as a relatively high level of trust in the local capacity to solve conflicts. It could also be taken as a trusted system because of its perennial, traditional nature but not necessarily because of its proven effectiveness.

Interestingly, the next question (Question 29) attracted the highest number of responses of all of the survey questions: "We are capable of solving our problems mostly by ourselves and go to court only if we need more help." The same scale was used. In Phidim, only one student (of 105) did not answer, and in Taplejung there were only 10 (of 132). Counting those who answered 1 to 6, the highest marks were 5.1 in Phidim and 4.9 in Taplejung, both in 2014.

| Capable of solving conflict mostly by ourselves | Phidim 2012 | Phidim 2013 | Phidim 2014 | Taplejung 2012 | Taplejung 2013 | Taplejung 2014 |
|---|---|---|---|---|---|---|
| Average mark | 3.6 | 5.1 | 5.1 | 3.7 | 4.4 | 4.9 |

This shows, firstly, that the belief in, or experience of, the local capability of solving conflicts has grown or remained strong over the three years at both sites. An unusually high percentage in the "very true" category (6) points to the perception of a local capacity to handle social conflicts by the population itself, mostly through trusted persons such as leaders and elders. We may conclude that despite the fratricidal violence during the insurgency and the political divides that took place in neighborhoods and families, there has been some resilience as to the capacity of solving local conflicts (which is an element of governance). The data also shows a respect by the younger generation (respondents were students) for traditional means of conflict resolution that involve trusting the older generation to act out of wisdom.

However, a cross-checking question (Question 35) was given afterwards. Students were asked to select one of three possibilities: "My preferred conflict resolution process is..." The responses in percentages for 2014 are shown here.

| My preferred form of conflict resolution: | Phidim 2014 % | Taplejung 2014 % |
|---|---|---|
| Community elders | 30 | 23 |
| Trained mediators | 26 | 32 |
| Legal topical experts | 44 | 45 |

Although Question 29 had shown a high level of trust in local, traditional means of conflict resolution and respondents would only take a case to court as last resort, Question 35 on the other hand showed that the same people would trust legal topical experts in solving an issue more than other methods. This contradiction may be explained by 1) the possibility to have ambiguity in our thinking and choices (*i.e.*, both may be true at the same time; and 2) the reason for remaining confident in traditional methods may be due to the fact that they do not cost anything. People might prefer, ideally, to use the law and refer to topical experts but scarce availability and high costs make them refer to cheaper, available and traditional methods (with which, overall, they are satisfied). As life becomes more technocratic and issues require greater knowledge of complex systems, resulting conflicts of development and change will probably be increasingly entrusted to certified professionals. Such knowledge, however, should be made transparent and accessible to all at each phase of any conflict so as to propagate capacity in good governance at grassroots levels also. After all, it is the conflict-owners who should become able to co-find and apply the solutions.

*Democracy*, Question 39 (red, perception/experience): "I feel free to contribute to the improvement of structures of democracy to the degree that I choose." On the same scale of 1 to 6, the averages in 2014 were 4.6 in Phidim and 3.8 in Taplejung, both above the midpoint.

It is interesting that the marks regarding "feeling free" to contribute to the improvement of democracy show a higher awareness or willingness of involvement than the real actions requested with Questions 10–14. Among other interpretations, this may point to an intellectual readiness that is not followed by action, or it may point to the propensity of students to engage for democracy in a non-typical political action such as through NGO or CBO activities. Civil society activities may have a greater attraction for many people than more politically-orientated activities.

*Political Peace,* Question 44 (red, perception/experience): "In my region, violent sub-groups are brought to the mainstream by peaceful political leaders." In 2014, the average mark was 3.5 in Phidim and 2.8 in Taplejung (on the scale of 1–6). Reflecting the marks given by the respondents, discussions, workshops and various other focus groups in the region brought to the fore that the heads of political parties themselves had not demonstrated peace leadership. Generally speaking, citizens felt sad to have "leaders choosing the path of political dispute instead of uniting the country to rebuild itself after the hurtful decade of 1996–2006."

Question 45 (red, perception/experience) asked: "I experience more political peace than one year ago." Averages were:

| More political peace than one year ago | Phidim 2012 | Phidim 2013 | Phidim 2014 | Taplejung 2012 | Taplejung 2013 | Taplejung 2014 |
|---|---|---|---|---|---|---|
| Average mark | 3.3 | 3.7 | 3.8 | 2.6 | 4 | 3.8 |

We observe, as with the experience of "more social peace than one year ago" in the SE portion of the questionnaire, that there is a constant improvement each year with a slight dip in the third year in Taplejung regarding GG. This reinforces the assumption that the respondents felt increasingly more at peace in their society, a reflection of the impact of the peace process.

Question 46a (green, action/peace engagement), "I am engaged in activities that foster political peace and good governance" gave the following averages for 2013 and 2014:

| Engaged in political peace & GG | Phidim 2013 | Phidim 2014 | Taplejung 2013 | Taplejung 2014 |
|---|---|---|---|---|
| Average mark | 4.4 | 4.6 | 3.5 | 3.8 |

Over 50% of the young Nepali surveyed thus say that they are involved in GG and peace fostering activities.

Question 46b (green) asked for qualitative information: "These are some of the activities I am engaged in…" Among the many answers, here are a few samples:

"I am doing social work."
"I am studying to be able to contribute."
"I follow the law."
"I link with authorities to improve social activities I am interested in."
"I am working with different organizations to improve society."
"I participate in awareness programs."
"I want to eliminate bad customs in my society."
"I want to help aged and disabled people."
"I work for the educational department."
"I am working to uproot untouchability."
"I work in poverty alleviation."
"I work in a cooperative."

In 2014, one year before the present constitution, an ultimate question was added to the GG portion of the questionnaire. It read: "If Nepal's politicians in Kathmandu do not create the Nepali state that I want with the constitution that I want, I would be willing to …"

a) "Wait until they do and live my life the best way I can." There was no possibility for "I don't know," and 18 students did not answer. Of those responding, 49% answered "yes" and 51% said "no."
   Those who answered "no" could continue with the following options:
b) To "take some action, for example":

   i) "Initiate public discussions to influence the government." 44 students said "yes" (79%) and 12 students said "no" (21%).

   ii) "Join a civil disobedience movement." 23 students said "yes" (46%) and 27 students said "no" (54%).

iii) "Risk my life to bring about change." 17 students said "yes" (35%) and 32 students said "no" (65%).

It would be interesting to follow up on this data by conducting further research with students, such as probing the motives and degree of motivation of the 17 students who expressed a willingness to risk their lives. A research question could be whether this willingness may be transformed – through peace education on B3 and i3 concepts and practices – into influential and direct actions that secure peaceful societal advancement without entailing risks to lives (their own and those of other people).

### *Synopsis of GG Questionnaire Results*

The results show that respondents have understood the importance of good governance and were keen to have it developed. They felt unsure as to the methods and practicalities and did not fully trust their elders or their leaders to manage this knowledge gap. They also felt disconcerted by their 1) lack of knowledge and 2) lack of empowerment at a personal level.

The respondents were keen to learn and to contribute in every way they could. Although sometimes shy in classrooms at first, they did express their opinions freely, albeit the young men much more so than the young women. During focus groups with older adults and in sessions with local politicians, there were fewer women than men in numbers but these women spoke as openly and as clearly as the men.

Often, the students in class in Phidim expressed sadness at not knowing about the world and "how things work." There is a wish to understand the methods of good governance, and how to solve problems that are filled with political, social and economic complexities. While a culture of village life and respect for the elders was appreciated, there was an aspiration for managerial capability that motivated students to learn about methods and processes. They felt frustrated in not knowing where to turn to learn this. Their trust in "mediators," *i.e.*, individuals who traveled through Nepal in the years after the signing of the Peace Agreement, and in the effectiveness of the Local Peace Committees as agents of harmonization remained modest. They wanted practical, solid methodologies of democratic governance.

Despite the fact that the local democracy between 2006 and 2014 (and until the time of publishing) was very indirect, we saw that a large majority of the student body felt free to contribute to the improvement of structures of democracy. We may conclude that the perception of individual liberty to participate is high, perhaps a reflection of the efforts to engage the population in the many dialogues towards constitution-making. This may also echo the fact that, due to remoteness, local day-to-day governance decisions continue to be handled directly by the inhabitants themselves. While being uninformed about technocratic processes of governance, the typical culture of community with a strong and shared stewardship of the local area is certainly not devoid of governance. It is simply waiting for the next level of organizational development, through managerial knowledge and direct democracy via local elections.

### *An Observation on Governance Participation in Panchthar*

Participation, we recall, can be either direct or through intermediate institutions and representatives. The participation component of governance ensures that the most vulnerable groups in society are brought into the decision-making process. This is made possible through upholding the principles of liberty of association and freedom of expression. It is regulated via an organized civil society that is accountable to its members, beneficiaries, stakeholders and other groups indirectly impacted upon.

In the span of time between 2011 and 2014 (I had been introduced to Phidim and Ilam[49] in 2010), I observed a large increase in participation in governance. Year-on-year, activities related to the development of the district had increased in scope and in scale. In the town of Phidim, particularly after becoming a municipality, buildings for state administration and for private enterprise literally sprang from the ground. Lateral roads intended for years were now nearing completion. The fresh water project for households, dormant despite secured budgets from the Asian Development Bank (ADB), was reaching completion in 2015. The various meeting halls and seminar rooms in local hotels, sadly empty in earlier years, were now continuously booked with this or that committee or commission debating some important local issue. I had to wait a week before obtaining an appointment

[49] Ilam is the district below Panchthar, also in the far east of Nepal. Its lower hills and pleasant climate are favorable for tea plantations. To the south, Ilam borders on Terai, the flat and fertile land contiguous to the northern Indian plains. The highway going north in far-eastern Nepal starts in Jhapa (Terai) and crosses Ilam, then Panchthar, and finally reaches the mountains ofTaplejung.

with a dignitary whereas previously it would have been possible to just walk into the person's office, be invited to sit down and explain my purpose on the spur of the moment. The reason was that the Chief District Officer, the District Development Officer and other senior administrators were constantly visiting the field, listening to the people in order to make good decisions. As will be explained later in the book, the education branch in Panchthar received a large boost when the District Education Officer, Gyan Mani Nepal, ensured that all schools would become "Zones of Peace" – reflecting the epitome of good governance within a State administration in the name of peace.

This buzz of activity was gripping the little bazaar between the hills of Ilam and the mountains of Taplejung, and it was founded on growing awareness and ability. Time and again I would hear that this or that group of people was out to receive training (agricultural bank team, women's co-operatives, water and irrigation team, etc.). So while on the one hand, good governance was still weak and largely unknown, it was nevertheless developing slowly, naturally, discreetly – and unabated.

Firstly, local NGOs were starting to give explicit "awareness-raising" and "informal training" on good governance at the grassroots level. Secondly, the overall capacity-building taking place in Nepal since the CPA was finally reaching into the plains and hills. Thirdly, the chief officers were themselves on a steep learning curve, having understood that developing the rural areas would guarantee the advancement of their country – and that they were personally accountable for this. Fourthly, the Nepali citizenry was realizing that it is fully able to debate, dialogue, find consensus and make intelligent decisions based on data, common sense and a fair vision of the future. The GG instruments may seem like complex technocracy at first and require knowledge certification, yet they still need to be applied by healthy minds and inclusive hearts. And that – of all things – is abundantly available in Nepal if people are given the chance to co-run their affairs. This is half of Nepal's future success criteria. What comes next is an egalitarian and empowered local democracy via local elections and the concrete application of checks and balances[50] by and upon the elected administrators.

50 "Checks and balances" is a self-regulated embedded system in any large organization or structure (such as a local or national government) whereby each branch automatically restrains one another from abusing its power.

## *Concluding Discussion*

Good governance is a major instrument for peace. Transparency means that rules and regulations are discussed and concluded in open forums (direct democracy) or by representatives who will reach agreement in committees (indirect democracy). Following this, the enforcement of decisions is consequential as relevant information and justification for the decisions are openly disclosed (*i.e.*, ignorance of the law is no excuse, providing the law is debated, passed, communicated, followed and enforced – to and for all concerned).

Boston *et al.* have discussed levels of ethical behaviors and gathered significant *Transparency Indicators for Public Policies.*[51] Of these, we cite four as examples:

a) Level of perceived corruption among politicians and public officials (Corruption Perception Index of Transparency International, 2008).
b) Four ethical behavior indicators: the extent of belief that it is justifiable to cheat on taxes, accept bribes, claim government benefits without entitlement, and not pay fares on public transport (Fifth wave of the World Value Survey, 2004–2008).
c) Extent of belief whether "most people can be trusted" (Fifth Wave of the World Values Survey, 2004–2008).
d) Accounting standards measuring the quality of accounts of leading companies based on indicators from an IMF working paper (De Nicolo *et al.*, 2006).

Further dimensions of GG are effectiveness, efficiency and economy – the three "Es" central to GG. The purpose of institutionalized processes and procedures is to produce results for the good of citizens. Governance is a continuous effort to seek and find a dynamic balance between the fulfillment of both universal and particular needs, as well as the allocation or re-distribution of available means and resources. This includes the practice of sustainability in the use of environmental resources, which aims to not produce waste.

Individuals who are paid by the state to seek and find such a dynamic equilibrium are required to act through programs and react to events with the most efficient time management. This is understood as the *responsiveness* element of GG.

---

[51] Boston *et al.* (2010), 203.

Not only individual governors but all staff of governmental institutions, and of public and private enterprises, are accountable to the general public. This *accountability* depends on the implementation of the rule of law and on agreed measures of transparency. It also depends on the ethical consciousness of each individual.

Good governance recognizes that there are varied opinions, needs and interests in any society, and that mechanisms of equilibrium and mediation are required to manage a dynamic and evolving consensus. The interest of the whole should also be achieved by responding to the interests of particular individuals and groups, yet to the degree that it does not jeopardize the rights and the achievements of other groups. This refers to the *consensus-orientation* within GG. Furthermore, such an equilibrium depends on the cultural, social and historical contexts of a society and cannot be transposed from one country's system into another's.

*Equity* and *inclusiveness* are key drivers in GG. It is important that all groups and sub-groups in a society experience themselves as belonging to and counting for its creation and maintenance. Feelings of exclusion can lead to depression and to violence. Therefore, good governance is about ensuring that no one is sidelined from the center or mainstream of society, especially people who already suffer from some vulnerability.

The rule of law, to be understood as a comprehensive legal framework for a whole country, qualifies the duties and the rights of all citizens. When enforced impartially, it protects all people from the violation of their rights, referring to their constitution, national laws and international conventions. It therefore relies on an independent and impartial judiciary as well as incorruptible national security and police forces.

Besançon, writing for the World Peace Foundation, explains that "the practice of good governance distinguishes successful democratic nations from states which do little for their people."[52] Governance can be rated through many critical public services intended to benefit all citizens, such as the impartial application of the rule of law, the provision of security, the freedom to express political opinions, the freedom to create employment for oneself and others or to enter into employment created by others, the possibility to access education and training programs as a child or adult, and unhindered access to health and other services.

52 Besançon (2003).

Afesis-Corplan, a South-African NGO with the aim to "achieve good governance and sustainable settlements through participatory methods that empower poor communities,"[53] developed with the help of the German GTZ and the Good Governance Learning Network a Good Governance Survey (GGS) in 2008. It surveys the views of elected local government representatives, officials, citizens and civil society actors in the following areas: public participation and consultation, transparency, decision-making, disclosure, service delivery, corruption, systems and structures.

Good governance also encourages a context of "partnership networks," in which the quality of relations between local players and the instruments used among them will largely determine local development outcomes.[54] The OECD makes a distinction between *good vertical governance* and *good horizontal governance*. Vertical governance aims to avoid gaps between local schemes and national policies. Horizontal governance seeks to encourage cross-scale learning among institutions, departments and other stakeholders engaged in local and regional governments. Both should work towards integration and mutual benefit:

> [...] locally-led or bottom-up where local initiatives influence national action and nationally-led or top-down where enabling frameworks empower local players. The most promising frameworks combine the two into hybrid models of policy dialogue where the lessons learnt are used to modify and fine-tune enabling frameworks and disseminated horizontally, achieving more efficient local implementation of [...] strategies.[55]

Importantly, GG is a lot about solving problems and managing conflicts with as much win-win as possible – at each administrative level. This involves many stakeholders, those concerned by issues directly and those who experience the consequential trickle-down or lateral-transversal impacts thereof. Mediation is a key skill inherent in GG, securing peace despite dilemmas and controversies, divergences and unavoidable conflicts of interest.

---

[53] http://www.afesis.org.za/

[54] OECD (2005), 45.

[55] Corfee-Morlot *et al*. (2009)

## 3. The Third Dimension: Sustainable Economic Development (SED)

Here the premise states that "the more *peace education* takes place, the more *sustainable economic development* will be." This view concerns the world as a whole, not just single (developing) economies, because the interdependencies of production, environmental impact, employment, mobility, financial stability and living standards are systemically linked between the West and the East, the North and the South. In a global village, sustainable development – *i.e.*, regulated and balanced economic life within a framework of governance that aims to secure social equity for all of humanity – ultimately concerns every worker, unemployed person, household, enterprise, institution and government.

We have discussed *social peace* and *political peace*. We now turn to the third variable, *economic peace*, which implies that all human beings can have the economic security that guarantees decent work or decent living. In a system where economic peace is central, there are no ultra-poor and people do not fear for their survival. Such a premise may imply that the ultra-rich have voluntarily relinquished excessive and exclusive privileges that consequentially push others into poverty.

Our logic, therefore, is: peace education teaches the principles and practices of equidistance between one's happiness and that of others, one's security and that of others, one's life fulfillment and that of others. At all levels of the curriculum in national schools and especially in universities and business schools, the concepts and methods of resource use, sectoral development, industrial production, commercial exchange, waste management and distribution of work need to be placed into a paradigm of peaceful stewardship. The intelligence of our engineers, practitioners and inventors should be at the service of humanity's healthy development – everywhere.

Sustainable economic development is by nature embedded within a framework of good governance that is conducive to social peace. For this, classic economic schools teaching economic equilibrium for a small planet which will soon have nine billion inhabitants must reconsider their fundamental hypotheses and beliefs that "resources are scarce." The very notion of scarcity – based on perceptions of lack, attitudes of fear and behaviors of dominion – engages actors to fight and scrape as much as possible to keep their own interests fulfilled and whenever possible their economy superior to that of others. Such schools of thought require a drastic overhaul, in richer and poorer countries alike, to recognize that the definitions of sustainability, development and economy have to be based on principles of shared, regulated, systemically renewed abundance.

Nepal, at the time of study, was the poorest country in South Asia and one of the least developed countries in the world. The causes for this and four strategic drivers for development are presented in my previous book.[56] The part of the survey that focused on the SED dimension, the third component of the PACE formula, asked the students for their experience, beliefs, actions and knowledge regarding economic development in their lives and in the region they live in. The range of questions covered their understanding of how an economic system can be sustainable, their belief in developing economically, their knowledge of resource wealth in their local area, their attitude towards cooperatives and micro-finance (traditional small- to medium-scale economic entities and means in the region), their inclination towards social enterprises, their interest in vocational training, their attitude towards "voluntary simplicity"[57] and whether they experienced more economic peace than a year earlier.

### *Selected Results: Sustainable Economic Development*

We take some samples from the SED portion of the questionnaire[58] to reflect upon the students' perception of, and participation in, the economic development of Nepal. The notion of sustainability was discussed during classes. To start with, we asked whether the students experienced economic development personally and believed that their local area could develop in comparison to the reality of previous generations. We also asked if the students felt interested in, and capable of, participating in a local sustainable

---

56 Duquesne (2011).

57 *Voluntary Simplicity*: a leading principle and pragmatic equalizer for poverty alleviation. The virtue and necessity of simplicity, while originally aimed at re-establishing sanity in the overly consuming rich countries, may prove appropriate for developing economies as well. See Elgin, D., *Voluntary Simplicity and The Living Universe* (1981) and *Voluntary Simplicity: Toward a Way of Life that is Outwardly Simple, Inwardly Rich* (1993), New York: Quill Books. These books are seminal works in the discussion about sustainable ways of living.

58 Sources for the design of this part of the questionnaire were: Indicators of Sustainable Development (UN), OECD, IISD, Encyclopedia of Earth, Global Urban Development (GUD), World Bank, SERI, Chemonics, ILO and Mindlab.

economy. The latter point links this B3 variable to the locus of control variable (loc) of i3 and refers to the immediate and direct connection between an *individual's* belief and concrete action towards the creation of a *collective* sustainable economy.

We asked the students to tell us about the sources of income in their families, which may be via parents, family members working abroad or any type of activity that flowed into the economic capacity of their immediate households. In 2014, 108 students participated in the SED questionnaire in Phidim and 129 in Taplejung. The introductory question asked them to complete the following: "As a family, we earn our living through…" by responding "yes" or "no" to eight possibilities. Between 15 and 26 students at either campus did not answer at least one of the eight options. Here are the results, in real numbers and percentages:

Phidim (2014): "As a family, we earn our living through… "

| | | YES | % | NO | % |
|---|---|---|---|---|---|
| a) | Remittances from family members working abroad | 42 | 45.7 | 50 | 54.3 |
| b) | Selling the produce of our land or crafts work | 56 | 60.9 | 36 | 39.1 |
| c) | Running our own business | 49 | 52.7 | 44 | 47.3 |
| d) | Public employment | 24 | 27.3 | 64 | 72.7 |
| e) | Private employment | 41 | 46.1 | 48 | 53.9 |
| f) | Cooperative/collective employment | 23 | 27.1 | 62 | 72.9 |
| g) | Letting property | 11 | 12.6 | 76 | 87.4 |
| h) | State allowance | 9 | 10.2 | 79 | 89.8 |

Taplejung (2014): "As a family, we earn our living through… "

| | | YES | % | NO | % |
|---|---|---|---|---|---|
| a) | Remittances from family members working abroad | 37 | 32.7 | 76 | 67.3 |
| b) | Selling the produce of our land or crafts work | 72 | 60.5 | 47 | 39.5 |
| c) | Running our own business | 49 | 45.8 | 58 | 54.2 |
| d) | Public employment | 33 | 31.7 | 71 | 68.3 |
| e) | Private employment | 40 | 38.5 | 64 | 61.5 |
| f) | Cooperative/collective employment | 22 | 20.6 | 85 | 79.4 |
| g) | Letting property | 11 | 10.7 | 92 | 89.3 |
| h) | State allowance | 12 | 11.7 | 91 | 88.3 |

In both Phidim and in Taplejung, we see that the main source of living is by selling the produce of land or crafts work. This confirms the reality of agriculture being the central source of subsistence in both districts. That the letting of property is a little higher in Phidim than in Taplejung may be a reflection of a slightly higher standard of living. In both cases, however, it is not a large source of income. Remittances from abroad are higher in Phidim and are the fourth source of income generation after the running of a family's business and private employment. This pattern is observable in Taplejung also.

An additional question asking students to name other sources of economic livelihood was regularly answered with "farming." While this can be a repetition of "selling the produce of our land or crafts work" to some extent, it may also refer to self-sustenance without any sale of surplus produce.

The following question asked the students to rate how their families perceived their own economic situations. This involved choosing only one of five categories. Here are the results in real numbers and percentages:

| Family Perceptions of Economic Situations (2014) | Phidim<br>108 students | Taplejung<br>129 students |
|---|---|---|
| a) Not enough to live on<br>*Basic needs remain unmet/suffer from cold or hunger* | 10<br>(9.3%) | 16<br>(12.4%) |
| b) Barely enough to live on<br>*Can afford no extras besides basic nutrition and home upkeep* | 33<br>(30.6%) | 36<br>(27.9%) |
| c) Enough to live on<br>*Basic needs met and small extras possible sometimes* | 32<br>(29.6%) | 43<br>(33.3%) |
| d) Comfortably<br>*Can afford to meet own needs, some needs of others, and some luxuries* | 18<br>(16.7%) | 12<br>(9.3%) |
| e) Well and enjoy surplus<br>*Can renew/upgrade components of our living, afford technological objects and new clothing, travel as we please, give as we please with no thought of personal constraint* | 8<br>(7.4%) | 6<br>(4.7%) |
| n/a | 7<br>(6.5%) | 16<br>(12.4%) |

Comparing the results from Phidim and Taplejung for all three years, we have the following data in percentages:

| | 2012 (%) | | 2013 (%) | | 2014 (%) | |
|---|---|---|---|---|---|---|
| Actual respondents | Phidim (124 of 132) | Taplejung (135 of 139) | Phidim (76 of 80) | Taplejung (62 of 70) | Phidim (101 of 108) | Taplejung (113 of 129) |
| Suffer | 22.0 | 8.6 | 13.8 | 12.9 | 9.3 | 12.4 |
| Barely enough | 46.2 | 40.3 | 32.5 | 32.9 | 30.6 | 27.9 |
| Enough | 18.9 | 38.8 | 30.0 | 31.4 | 29.6 | 33.3 |
| Comfortable | 5.3 | 5.8 | 15.0 | 7.1 | 16.7 | 9.3 |
| Surplus | 1.5 | 3.6 | 3.8 | 4.3 | 7.4 | 4.7 |
| n/a | 6.1 | 2.9 | 5.0 | 11.4 | 6.5 | 12.4 |

Over the three years, the percentage of Phidim students responding "not enough/suffer" decreased from 22% to 14% to 9% (in rounded numbers). In the category "barely enough," we observe a decrease from 46% to 33% to 31%. The "enough" category rises from 19% to 30% and is constant in the following year. The "comfortable" category shows an increase from 5% to 15% to 17%. The "living well and have surplus" category shows an increase from 2% to 4% to 7%.

Taplejung, on the other hand, shows an increase of economic suffering and then a slight decline, a decrease of "barely enough," and a decrease followed by a small increase of "enough." It also shows an increase of "comfortable" and a slight increase of "surplus."

Allowing for imperfections such as partly new individual respondents each year, varying sizes of population samples and different styles of translating by assisting teachers, we must interpret the data with caution. Yet we may suggest that this information reveals an overall trend towards economic improvement at both sites, with a sharper (factual or perceptual) improvement in Phidim. We may hypothesize that this is due to Phidim being closer to the south of the country (with easier access to larger towns in Terai and to India) and thus also to Kathmandu. Commercial and employment opportunities may reach Taplejung later due to greater physical distances. Taplejung hosts more tourists than Phidim as it has a small airport and is a starting point for trecks into the Himalayas; yet Phidim has a larger turnover of Nepali visitors with some kind of business or work motivation.

Question 2 (blue, belief/assumption) asked: "In my work life after college, I think I will not improve my economic development in Nepal because of insufficient good governance, including that of the labor market." The response scale ranged from 1 (not true at all) to 6 (very true). The results for 2014 were:

| I will not improve my economic development because of insufficient governance | 2014 (%) Phidim (89 responses) | Taplejung (105 responses) |
|---|---|---|
| 1 | 32.6 | 27.4 |
| 2 | 15.7 | 14.3 |
| 3 | 9.0 | 10.5 |
| 4 | 13.5 | 8.6 |
| 5 | 9.0 | 12.4 |
| 6 | 20.2 | 26.7 |

Beyond seeking an average here, the point of interest lies in the polarity between (1+2) and (5+6). We notice that many students in Taplejung strongly believe that they will not improve their economic life because of insufficient governance (5+6). On the other hand, a larger amount of students believe that they will increase their economic standard (1+2). What we do not know is whether they link their assumptions to their ability to bypass insufficient governance or because they assume that insufficient governance will diminish enough to enable economic development for them personally.

Question 3 (blue, belief/assumption) asked: "In my work life after college, I think I will not improve my economic development in Nepal because of lack of opportunities in the country." Again, the scale was 1 (not true at all) to 6 (very true).

| I will not improve my economic development because of lack of opportunities in the country | 2014 (%) Phidim (90 responses) | Taplejung (105 responses) |
|---|---|---|
| 1 | 25.6 | 18.6 |
| 2 | 11.1 | 10.8 |
| 3 | 8.9 | 17.6 |
| 4 | 13.5 | 10.8 |
| 5 | 14.4 | 12.7 |
| 6 | 25.6 | 29.4 |

Here, too, we have data that is polarized between extremes, especially for Phidim, and a stronger agreement with the question-statement in Taplejung. We may assume very different views on how the younger generation intends to tackle their own economic development. Some will be positive and gather strength to try new things (such as going abroad), others will be negative and see no opportunity around them.

Question 4 (blue, belief/assumption) aimed to cross-check the previous questions. It stated: "In my work life after college, I believe I will be able to realize my goals, at least partially, and enjoy personal economic development." The same scale was used: 1 (not true at all) to 6 (very true).

| | 2012 (%) | | 2013 (%) | | 2014 (%) | |
|---|---|---|---|---|---|---|
| I will be able to enjoy personal economic development | Phidim 132 students - 6 n/a | Taplejung 139 students - 1 n/a | Phidim 80 students - 4 n/a | Taplejung 70 students - 15 n/a | Phidim 108 students - 14 n/a | Taplejung 129 students - 24 n/a |
| 1 | 7.6 | 2.2 | 6.3 | 11.4 | 4.6 | 9.3 |
| 2 | 2.3 | 4.3 | 2.5 | 8.6 | 3.7 | 6.2 |
| 3 | 6.8 | 10.8 | 11.3 | 5.7 | 7.4 | 7.0 |
| 4 | 10.6 | 18.0 | 8.8 | 11.4 | 12.0 | 10.9 |
| 5 | 22.7 | 23.0 | 21.3 | 12.9 | 11.1 | 13.2 |
| 6 | 45.5 | 41.0 | 45.0 | 28.6 | 48.1 | 34.9 |
| n/a | 4.5 | 0.7 | 5.0 | 21.4 | 13.0 | 18.6 |
| Average mark | 4.8 | 4.8 | 4.8 | 4.2 | 4.9 | 4.4 |

We notice that the mark 6 (very true) has the highest percentage of responses each year at both sites. We also note, despite a small drop for Taplejung, that the average marks are all above 4 and thus may indicate a general belief (even if not extremely strong) in one's aptitude to realize one's economic goals, at least partially. We cannot speak of a negative, doom-like view of the students towards their country. Rather, they see themselves – more than not – as future beneficiaries (maybe creators) of greater economic opportunities.

Questions 9–11 dealt with the topic of cooperatives. We wanted to gauge the attitude of students towards this form of economic entity, which is an important feature of livelihood in Nepal. Question 9 (green, action) asked "Are you a member of a cooperative?" These are the results for 2013 and 2014:

| Are you a member of a cooperative? | | | | | | | |
|---|---|---|---|---|---|---|---|
| Phidim (2013) | | Taplejung (2013) | | Phidim (2014) | | Taplejung (2014) | |
| 80 students - 1 n/a | | 70 students - 4 n/a | | 108 students - 5 n/a | | 129 students - 4 n/a | |
| Yes | No | Yes | No | Yes | No | Yes | No |
| 21.5% | 78.5% | 24.2% | 75.8% | 26.2% | 73.8% | 24.8% | 75.2% |

Question 10 (green, action) asked of those who answered "no" in Question 9: "Would you like to join a cooperative, or other cooperatives, if there is a chance?"

| Would you like to join a cooperative, or other cooperatives, if there is a chance? | | | | | | | |
|---|---|---|---|---|---|---|---|
| Phidim (2013) | | Taplejung (2013) | | Phidim (2014) | | Taplejung (2014) | |
| 80 students - 12 n/a | | 70 students - 20 n/a | | 108 students - 28 n/a | | 129 students - 36 n/a | |
| Yes | No | Yes | No | Yes | No | Yes | No |
| 92.6% | 7.4% | 92.0% | 8.0% | 92.5% | 7.5% | 95.7% | 4.3% |

Question 11 (green, action) asked: "Would you like to start a cooperative as soon as you have the chance?"

| Would you like to start a cooperative as soon as you have the chance? | | | | | | | |
|---|---|---|---|---|---|---|---|
| Phidim (2013) | | Taplejung (2013) | | Phidim (2014) | | Taplejung (2014) | |
| 80 students - 18 n/a | | 70 students - 19 n/a | | 108 students - 32 n/a | | 129 students - 41 n/a | |
| Yes | No | Yes | No | Yes | No | Yes | No |
| 83.9% | 16.1% | 76.5% | 23.5% | 86.8% | 13.2% | 84.1% | 15.9% |

We see from the results that, by and large, roughly two-thirds of the respondents were not members of cooperatives in 2013 and 2014. This may be due to the fact that they were students. Had the question been asked about their mothers or fathers, maybe the answers would have changed. Another reason may be that cooperatives are too few in number or are made insufficiently attractive to potential younger members.

On the other hand, students overwhelmingly said that they would join a cooperative (in the future) if they had the chance. This leads us to think that there is a certain level of trust in this form of entity in terms of providing economic security or return on interest – in which case, we may assume that cooperatives are seen as appropriate and worthwhile.

When the same students were asked if they would take it upon themselves to create a cooperative, the response was more measured. Still, in Phidim, 52 students in 2013 and 66 in 2014 were willing to consider taking a leadership role and starting a cooperative, while in Taplejung 39 students in 2013 and 74 in 2014 said the same. This result indicated some internal locus of control at the individual level.

During the classes on economic peace, mention was made of the role played by "social enterprises" – their commonalities but also their differences to cooperatives, as pure players. The next question in the survey aimed to test the propensity for entrepreneurship, especially in view of linking the Big 3 (SED, GG and SED).

Question 12 (green, action) asked: "I intend to start a social enterprise." The results for 2014 are as follows:

| I intend to start a social enterprise. | | | |
|---|---|---|---|
| Phidim (2014) 108 students - 42 n/a | | Taplejung (2014) 129 students - 49 n/a | |
| YES | NO | YES | NO |
| 45.5% | 54.5% | 47.5% | 52.5% |

The very high number of n/a shows the difficulty of imagining what a social enterprise may be if it is not a cooperative. Even if that is understood, it remained difficult for students to identify with it due to the absence of local examples. Nonetheless, 30 students in Phidim and 38 students in Taplejung said they could imagine themselves starting a social enterprise.

Question 16 (red, perception/experience) turned to the concept of voluntary simplicity and asked the students: "To me, voluntary simplicity is ... " Students could select only one of the five answers below, with percentages given for their 2014 responses:

a) Not relevant for Nepal, because the country is too poor to consider simplicity as attractive
Phidim: 20.4%; Taplejung: 27.1%
b) Unrealistic, because people want to catch up with the consumption level of the richer countries
Phidim: 14.8%; Taplejung: 13.2%
c) A necessary practice for our country to balance poverty reduction and new, unchecked affluence
Phidim: 37.0%; Taplejung: 27.1%
d) Crucial for Nepal as for all countries to manage the planet's resources sustainably together
Phidim: 13.0%; Taplejung: 7.8%
e) Do not know + n/a
Phidim: 14.8%; Taplejung: 24.8%

This question was quite demanding and the high level of n/a is understandable. A predominant opinion at both sites was that voluntary simplicity is a necessary practice to manage poverty reduction in correlation with a growing middle class, *i.e.*, the old rich and the new rich should temper their personal ambitions in order to help the less fortunate. Another dominant opinion was that voluntary simplicity was not a valid concept for Nepal in view of the ubiquitous poverty and thus "simplicity" could not be equated with improvement. The idea of linking Nepal's managed growth and development via "enough is good" to the entire world's dire need for sustainable livelihood systems attracted the students' attention least.

Teaching peaceful economic development or, reversely, making economic development into a driver for peace, may consider paying homage to principles of voluntary simplicity. In a free world, anyone has the right to be an economic agent to the degree that he or she wants. Once the initial extra means have been gathered, it is not so difficult to use of the market rules to multiply them. What does matter, in order to avoid the traps of merchandise-hoarding and game corruption, is an ethical stance of fairness and redistribution linked to liberty itself. The willing self-restraint for the benefit of others – altruism – has to be taught via education, channeled through governance, possibly coerced through structures of constraint. As much as it calls for good management of collective wealth redistribution, sustainable economic development calls for individual economic containment or careful and caring dissemination on the basis of an informed conscience. In this way, the governance of wealth is also a preserver of peace.

Question 21 (red, perception/experience) inquired about the economic development of the students' local areas. The question was: "I evaluate economic development in my local area as follows..." As a sample, we reproduce results in percentages in Phidim (108 actual respondents) in 2014:

| I evaluate economic development in my local area as... | Non-existent | Very weak | Slowly developing | Developing fast | Very strong | Don't know |
|---|---|---|---|---|---|---|
| Trade and commercial exchanges | 6.5 | 21.3 | 48.1 | 8.3 | 4.6 | 11.1 |
| Farming (crops, teas, herbs, animals) | 0 | 13.9 | 35.2 | 30.6 | 11.1 | 9.3 |
| Road and infrastructure, construction, buildings | 1.9 | 17.6 | 31.5 | 29.6 | 6.5 | 13.0 |
| Energy production (wind, hydropower, solar, thermal ... ) | 3.7 | 19.4 | 35.2 | 22.2 | 3.7 | 15.7 |
| Water use (irrigation, fishing, drinking, household, ... ) | 2.8 | 17.6 | 30.6 | 25.0 | 12.0 | 12.0 |
| Factories, manufacturing, processing works | 19.4 | 28.7 | 24.1 | 12.0 | 6.5 | 9.3 |
| Forest produce | 1.9 | 17.6 | 27.8 | 23.1 | 17.6 | 12.0 |
| Tourism | 7.4 | 13.9 | 23.1 | 25.9 | 17.6 | 12.0 |

Indeed, this reflects a region where economic sectors are developing slowly. The manufacturing sector in the form of factories and processed produce is the least developed. No sector is attributed particularly high levels of strength, yet economic activity on the whole is increasing due to the building of roads, accessibility to loans, education and mobility. Providing there is political stability, the local economy seems able to maintain a sustainable development. This is the result of the hard work of Nepali people and of the long-term cooperation and assistance programs of agencies such as the World Bank, the Asia Development Bank and various foundations (of friendly governments and of private sources).

Question 25 (blue, belief/assumption) asked the students to complete the following sentence: "To me, economic peace is when..." Here are some samples of their answers:

"...there is no corruption in the process of economic development."

"...we introduce industry in our region."

"...when everyone gets opportunities for employment."

"...when people get their basic needs fulfilled."

"...when strong state leadership enforces (an) egalitarian economic system to avoid differences and abuse."

"...when the stewards of the country have scientific education and also behavioral education."

"When there is peace in the country, then there will be economic peace also."

"Within the next 5 years, I expect more economic peace in my country."

Question 26 (red, experience) asked: "I experience more economic peace in my local area than one year ago." This was a concluding question each year with each of the B3 variables. Once again, the responses range from 1 (not true at all) to 6 (very true). The longitudinal results are thus:

| | 2012 (%) | | 2013 (%) | | 2014 (%) | |
|---|---|---|---|---|---|---|
| I experience more economic peace than one year ago | Phidim 132 students - 10 n/a | Taplejung 139 students - 8 n/a | Phidim 80 students - 10 n/a | Taplejung 70 students - 12 n/a | Phidim 108 students - 15 n/a | Taplejung 129 students - 20 n/a |
| 1 | 22.7 | 16.5 | 12.5 | 22.9 | 11.1 | 17.8 |
| 2 | 10.6 | 14.4 | 17.5 | 17.1 | 6.5 | 15.5 |
| 3 | 16.7 | 13.7 | 10.0 | 11.4 | 13.0 | 11.6 |
| 4 | 15.2 | 15.8 | 21.3 | 11.4 | 10.2 | 14.7 |
| 5 | 14.4 | 15.1 | 11.3 | 11.4 | 17.6 | 10.1 |
| 6 | 12.9 | 18.7 | 15.0 | 8.6 | 27.8 | 14.7 |
| n/a | 7.6 | 5.8 | 12.5 | 17.1 | 13.9 | 15.5 |
| Average | 3.3 | 3.6 | 3.5 | 2.9 | 4.2 | 3.3 |

We note that Phidim shows a small increase in the perception of "more economic peace" year-on-year. Taplejung, on the other hand, shows a decrease in 2013 and a small increase in 2014, producing an average mark over the three years of slightly above 3.

Comparing the average marks in each year with those for the other B3 variables (SE and GG), we have the following data:

| B3 variables | 2012 average marks | | 2013 average marks | | 2014 average marks | |
|---|---|---|---|---|---|---|
| I experience more peace than one year ago | Phidim | Taplejung | Phidim | Taplejung | Phidim | Taplejung |
| SE | 4.2 | 3.7 | 3.8 | 3.2 | 4.3 | 3.9 |
| GG | 3.3 | 3.7 | 3.8 | 2.6 | 4.0 | 3.8 |
| SED | 3.3 | 3.6 | 3.5 | 2.9 | 4.2 | 3.3 |

While Phidim shows a slight increase of experiencing more peace across the dimensions than the year before, Taplejung remains modest in its experience. Low ratings (1 or 2) were seldom given, in a context that included the absence of violent conflict. However, growth of peace through SE, GG and SED was not gauged as strongly existent.

## *Synopsis of SED Questionnaire Results*

The young adult generation surveyed gave of itself the image of an economic standard where most thought there was "enough to live on" or at least "barely enough to live on," although the perception of "not having enough to live on" was not insignificant. A low percentage of "being at ease economically" grew slowly but continuously. In the pursuit of our study, much local travel took place along the tarred and dirt roads and on foot to very remote villages. Indeed, in the course of the four years in the region, signs of a slightly easier economic situation gradually came to the fore. Marketplaces are busier, new buses travel around filled to the brink, hotels have sprung up and mobile phones are in every pocket. Upward social mobility is slowly emerging. Subsistence from farming remains the fundamental economic reality, yet in many places there is a mix of individual and collective efforts at increased and diversified economic activities. Most farmers own some land and their survival is superior to that of the previous generations.[59]

[59] This is especially true of the south and east of Nepal and the region around Kathmandu.

Students showed an interesting division in their beliefs of whether they would be able to improve economically in their lives. A large proportion thought they would not, while an even larger group thought that they surely would. In between lay the spread-out views of more or less certainty. This is indicative of some positive development whereby many young adults have the feeling that their generation is upgrading in economic status, even if only a little. Considering their freedom to earn dollars abroad, to continue studying on campus or to create a business, a tacit new trust in the future is shown through the data, even if verbal expressions sometimes reflect an absence of direction, resentment at lack of opportunities and what may sometimes appear as the listing of convenient excuses for lingering procrastination. Interestingly, sharp students who were hungry to act, to let their dignity shine and to change the game were more vocal in Taplejung than in Phidim, although overall their data generally revealed more negative views.

The respondents showed an understanding and a respect for cooperatives as a valid form of economic entity. They did not value as much the notion of voluntary simplicity, although in hindsight the concept was difficult to understand deeply, especially without a course introduction into the topic (as was the case in Taplejung, where only short definitions were given by assisting teachers). Students could reflect upon the economic sectors of their region and their state of development. During discussions about "how to develop these," however, there was very little knowledge – or imagination – as to possible means or processes for economic growth.

The idea that sustainable economic development should be both a cause and a consequence of peace was clear in the minds of the students. That SED should be related to SE and GG was also obvious to them. What was not as evident in their reflection was the relationship between i3 and B3. The paramount responsibility of the individual at this crucial time of change in Nepal and the necessity to align peacemaking with economic development at an individual level (proactively) was hardly fathomable for some of them. Only a few in the class caught on to the actual meaning of the

The west and northwest of the country (as well as the higher hills that are not linked to the touristic mountain areas) suffer more from poverty. This was exemplified when the UNICEF office for Panchthar left Phidim in 2014 as the Development Indices for the Child became fulfilled in that district. It then moved to the west of the country to attend to more pressing needs there.

PACE formula. When they did, however, they became highly enthusiastic. This tells of the potential good in applying the formula more deeply over a longer period of time.

## *Cooperatives in Panchthar*

*Cooperatives have been instrumental in peace-building.*[60]

The Nepalese people have a long tradition – and competence – in cooperation and labor-sharing. In 2014, there were over 30,000 cooperatives in Nepal, many of them savings and credit cooperatives. Others are agricultural – animal-rearing, dairy, small farmers, coffee and tea – and there are also multipurpose, herbal, health, electricity, consumer, and science and technology cooperatives, and more. In order to start a cooperative, 25 people are required to agree to a constitution and the establishment of rules. An office with functionaries, an accounting system, data management and pictorial proof are necessary prior to registration.

Cooperatives have grown in number and in professionalism, and despite the overall difficulty of Nepal in creating sustainable markets, efforts have sought to improve the links between production and distribution channels. The grassroots-level understanding of the value of cooperatives is evident, also thanks to training in the skills of administration, management and accounting as provided by the cooperatives' bureaus and by NGOs. At the ministerial level, cooperatives have long been recognized as an appropriate and natural way for Nepalis to create local economies. In 1953, the Department of Cooperatives (DOC) was established under the Ministry of Agriculture for Planning and Development.[61] In March 2014, the First National Cooperative Congress was organized with the collaboration of the Government of Nepal, Ministry of Cooperatives and Poverty Alleviation, National Cooperative Federation of Nepal, National Cooperative Development Board and Department of Cooperatives. In 2015, "the 18th SAARC summit held in Kathmandu recognized the potential of cooperatives in achieving inclusive, broad-based and sustainable economic growth and development, and called for sharing of experiences, expertise and best practices in this sector."[62]

60 See Adhikari (2013).

61 http://www.ncfnepal.com.np/historicalevents.html

In 2014, there were 75 active cooperatives in Panchthar, of which 24 were multipurpose, a growing trend. Many of them were savings and credit cooperatives. There was no – to date – housing cooperative. A talk with the head of the cooperative bureau in Phidim revealed another side of the coin: 220 cooperatives had been registered but two-thirds were inactive. This was a source of frustration and a loss of initial funds that had not borne fruit. The reasons for this were multiple: life changes with the departure of key people, non-productivity due to lack of leadership or effort, non-marketability (lack of profit and the members themselves were too poor to honor their membership), or corruption (obtaining the initial funds and misusing them).

The officer said that cooperatives deserve a lot more attention from the government and from funding sources. Due to a lack of investment in this sector, the poverty alleviation work – an active area for NGOs – started to receive funds to form cooperatives. As the NGOs themselves were able to become cooperatives, they competed with other local cooperatives. This competition shook the sector awake to manage its duties better, and "we have been able to act more effectively together as a result."[63]

Among the positive examples of blended self- and collective enterprise in Panchthar is the Deurali Multipurpose Cooperative. Established in 2007, there are four employees in the core group and 1,067 members, 734 of whom are women. Initially, two founders went to Japan and India to observe and learn from existing cooperatives. Then, they took a loan from a commercial bank, and developed the ability to provide the services of a commercial bank themselves, as a cooperative. Mostly, it acts as a loan provider, an enabling pool of loans and savings. It is an easily accessible alternative to banks, acting as a micro-financing provider.[64]

The cooperative gives preference to the poor, Dalits and people without collateral or documents. Members benefit in the following way: with the birth of a child (up to 2 children), the mother is given 2000 Nepali rupees (NPR). After a death, a member is given 5000 NPR and relatives receive 2000 NPR. In 2013, Deurali enjoyed the highest membership of all 75 cooperatives that were active in Panchthar. It has received recognition and the

62 *Ibid.*

63 Interview and conversations at the Cooperatives' Bureau, Phidim, 2014.

64 This is inspired by the Grameen Bank, founded by Muhammad Yunus, in Bangladesh (seminal business work with micro-finance) yet also adapted to local realities.

Excellency Award from the district office for cooperatives and also from the Nepal Rastra Bank.

Deurali's activities include mentoring the inception of new collective businesses such as vegetable wholesalers, fertilizers or other small ventures. By 2013, it had provided loans and coached 17 groups to start or expand their businesses, 320 ventures in farming, and 120 in businesses (*e.g.*, opening a small shop in a village). After an initial advisory phase they leave the business to act independently, only monitoring the financial repayment.

When interviewed, Deurali reported significant changes in the last few years. Business was increasing, and behaviors were changing as people became more entrepreneurial and more active. The connectivity to markets, however, is a real problem, and the groups are themselves responsible for tackling it. Some sell to Jhapa, some to Taplejung. Some sell to Naxal in India. There is little activity outside of this relatively small radius. Nothing goes to China. Further away, only some cheese and handicrafts will make it to the EU or the USA.

As for the impact of their work on peace, Deurali clearly responded that there is more social peace thanks to cooperatives. People report satisfaction – and gratefulness. "It is very important to work together, to share information. We are linking peace-building with the cooperative way of economic development. They are related to each other and, yes, we shall make this ever more explicit."[65]

## *Concluding Discussion*

SED is a pillar of societal peace and a core element of the peaceability formula. The interdependence between individual locus of control and economic development is particularly evident: people are responsible for their course of achievement and for turning effort into material and other gains. Should the circumstances be especially difficult, a person still has – potentially – the imagination and the learning quotient to find ways and means to overcome economic downturns and at least live a simple, even satisfying life. Social capital, for example through collective support in economic downturns, is important.

The relationship between SED and empathy may be a little more hidden. It calls for a premise of altruism whereby one can only truly benefit

[65] Interview and focus group in 2013.

from economic improvement (deeply and in the long-term) if others do so too. Therefore, the poverty of others is also one's personal concern. This logic becomes complicated if the person who is willing to share a gain borne of effort observes that the other has stayed in rudimentary conditions for lack of motivation or thrift. Empathy is more difficult given such observation or interpretation. One answer to this dilemma is to have SED taught in schools along with the preparation of young minds to grasp their personal responsibility in creating economic stability for themselves and for the community, with humanistic practices of sharing and redistribution. This is where peace education bears fruit at a societal level, including economic capability.

The link between SED and basic trust (bat) is also complex. It means that the individual economic agent "believes" – yes, even "perceives" – that the world, nature, systems, the universe is fundamentally a place of abundance. Creation of work is like creating a piece of art. This is a way of thinking and a way of being that is not yet taught in business schools, in Masters of Commerce or PhDs in Economics, but it is a field of research that is on the rise. What if there were enough – yes, plenty, to go around? What if poverty were absolutely unnecessary? Individuals who base the reasoning of their lives on such a premise are likely to be change-setters. Such perception points to a paradigm shift and can only happen through individuals. Economic sectors, in time, may reflect such a state of mind, rendering the hoarding of resources and most conflicts of interest at best obsolete, at least checked.

We recall that peaceability (*i.e.*, demonstrating peaceful behaviors) depends on the pre-condition of having one's basic needs met in the first place. The hierarchy of needs elaborated by Maslow[66] placed physiological needs – the most basic ones (food, water, air, sleep) – at the bottom of his pyramid, safety and security at the second level up, love and belonging in the third, esteem in the fourth and self-actualization at the top. Maslow further identified these four lower levels as "deficiency needs," meaning that – if not answered – they would lead to psychological disorder. The upper echelon, or "growth needs," could be attained only after having met the previous four.[67] Extrapolating Maslow's theory, the development of popu-

66 Maslow (1943).

67 Gonzalez-DeHass & Willems (2013), 310.

lations may be considered as following a similar pattern. The fulfillment of the minimal threshold of needs for a basic, decent and self-sufficient livelihood prevents social neurosis that sooner or later turns into psychotic violence – or gets instrumentalized as excuse for power-grabbing through violence.

A central political and economic question is whether the fulfillment of basic needs is provided through employment, individual enterprise or other means such as redistribution of (individual or common) surplus – a sort of welfare. A system of balance between demand and supply, seconded by instruments of regulation, make it possible for a wide range of providers to benefit from exchange, directly or indirectly. A vertical trickle-down effect of surplus generation is the expectation derived from profitability. In the case of Nepal, however, economic development has been a very rough road since the 1950s. Employment, enterprise, redistribution, demand, supply and regulation have been nearly absent for most of the population until very recently.

Collier, discussing causes of civil war, deduced that if we "halve the starting income of the country [we] double the risk of civil war."[68] If mass poverty is one factor among the causes of insurgencies, then economic development nust accelerate in order to be at peace – hence the importance of "not missing the boat"[69] and orientating globalization towards demarginalizing the poor.

The notion of sustainability also means refraining from jumping into any kind of development at any cost. Sustainable development suggests that emerging products and services fulfill a real demand, add value to the life of the users, maintain a non-damaging equilibrium (socially and environmentally) and contribute to a positive circulation and exchange of value to as many people as possible.[70] Reactive to evolutionary forces such as technology, population growth or competing structures of power governing human affairs, the answer to fulfilling needs has been following one tenet, mostly: that of economic growth by having as large a trade surplus as pos-

68 Collier (2007), 19.

69 *Ibid.*, 79.

70 Soubbotina (2004). Also See *Agenda 21*, the agreement adopted by nations participating in the Earth Summit in Rio de Janeiro, Brazil, in 1992. "21" refers to the 21$^{st}$ century. The non-binding agreement, orchestrated by the UN, specified a plan of action to apply sustainable development at international, national and local levels.

sible. Likewise at the micro level, the individual fulfillment of needs has been oriented towards individual economic surplus, considering "success" in life as financial earnings and social status above other factors (which is not aligned with the fundamental precepts of the sustainability paradigm).

The Basic Needs theory in the context of development was introduced by the International Labour Organization in 1976. One among the development theories, it advocates an approach that ensures "satisfying minimum levels of material needs such as consumption of food, shelter and clothing, and access to such essential public services as pure water, sanitation, public transport, health and education."[71] To meet the needs of the population, especially in poor regions, the "grow first/redistribute later" policy seems uncertain. An alternative may be to consider a "re-distribute first/grow later" strategy (*e.g.*, as development budgets by the central government, subsidies for sectors or individual benefits for citizens). If the government cannot afford this, international aid can help. Since it will most probably never suffice, the populations concerned would be advised to share resources at a local level and create themselves a livelihood that is increasingly sustainable. The necessity to create micro-economies that suffice for a decent living require commitment and hard work, and – in the case of the Nepali people – the desire to stay and build such local economies rather than labor in the Middle East to erect other people's buildings for $150 a month.[72]

How may we develop fairly? How can we rise above poverty and keep a healthy balance within and between the human and natural systems? How to raise economic chances in a just way? How to exploit the economic value of natural resources without damaging them and with a fair redistribution of the rewards? How can we establish economic peace?

The action research observed over four years whether the town of Phidim could become a "peace town," possibly twinning with peace towns

[71] Samater (1984), quoted in Jaffee (1998), 103.

[72] When the ILO defined basic needs as "the minimum standard of living which a society should set for the poorest groups of people," it was both welcome (Stewart (1985), 7) and criticized as a "materialistic" and "paternalistic" approach (Sen (1993), 30–53). Since then, a more synthetic view has emerged whereby the basic needs theory has learned from the structural strategies of the 1980s and 1990s by the World Bank and the IMF as much as from the ethnic and local politics of "place" by their opponents. It is possible to conceive of a blend between independent and interdependent local economics *and* active cooperation with national and global networks, within a framework of shared good governance.

in Germany and other countries. We encourage this observation to continue. SED can be used in the future as an indicator to link collective peaceability with practical instruments towards shared economic improvement. Social scientists, economists, province administrators, businesses, cooperatives and NGOs could consider the creation of a think tank at local level that statistically and qualitatively follows the reciprocal impact of GG, SED and SE over time. Highly valuable would be the tracing and proving of individual contributions and personal engagement as key factors for collective peace across all the variables.

# CHAPTER 4

# WORKING WITH SCHOOLS AND OTHER PARTNERS

In 2011, five years after the CPA was signed, not all schools were peaceful places. UN agencies were expressing strong concerns over attacks by activists and the frequency of days when schools had to remain closed. UNICEF was appealing to government, political parties and child-protection organizations to ensure that children in Nepal be allowed to learn, play and grow in an atmosphere free of violence and interference (like most countries, Nepal is a signatory of the Convention on the Rights of the Child). In a muddle of anger about unequal opportunities and accusations against political elites backed by foreign interests, there were also reports of vandalism against schools with English names.

This chapter covers four case studies comprising the activities performed by myself and the colleagues, supporters and friends I worked with over the four years of our joint action-research. During that time, we collaborated with two school establishments – one government or "community" school and one private "boarding" school in Phidim. Case studies 1 and 2 present the activities performed there, the third focuses on an NGO working with development programs and the fourth relates to the beginnings of a "peace trail" initiative. In all four cases, Nepali partners initiated or intensified peace actions especially for and in accompaniment to this research.

## 1. Shree Phidim School (Case Study 1)

Established in 1948, Shree Phidim Higher Secondary School (SPHSS) is the oldest school in Phidim. It is close to the bazaar, the busy town hub witnessing private construction works and the expansion of the water supply (a long-pending ADB-funded project). Such activities reflect times of peace. During the insurgency, development was impossible and the school was forced to remain closed (like local businesses and administrative offices) for many weeks each year. Between 1996 and 2006, the generation of pupils then aged 6 to 16 received no education that would lead to good employment or job-creation. Opportunities were absent. That generation – young men in particular and increasingly young women as well – is the one presently laboring abroad and sending remittances for the economic upkeep of their families.

Today, the school caters for primary, secondary and higher secondary levels. For the time being, classes IV-VII are conducted in Nepali. Higher secondary classes XI-XII provide business and management studies in English and Nepali, and science in English only. Altogether, 214 primary, 251 secondary and 107 higher secondary school-goers make up a student body of 572.

Mr. Bhandari, the Principal, gave his consent for our research activities to take place at the school. Vice-principal and English teacher Mr. Lawati agreed to guide students in conducting a small longitudinal study on the state of peace in the school in 2013 and 2014 via a simple survey. I gave several classes on the topic of peace, and a teachers' meeting was organized to make them aware of the study and ask for their cooperation. Together with the district court lawyer, Mr. Sikdel, a bilingual presentation on moral behavior, law-abiding and societal peace was given (jointly in English and Nepali) to the elder pupils, with the title of "Peace Matters."[73] A second lecture on "Preventive Reduction of Social and Home Violence" was planned but did not take place. Mr. Sikdel was a paralegal for the district during the years when the peace process included a sub-program on paralegal actions to address the many protracted injustices and enduring local conflicts as remnants of the insurgency; these were too many for the district court and a lawyer would have been too costly for the plaintiffs.

The insurgency had awakened a revolutionary political consciousness by and large absent in Nepal until then. To arouse motivation in little time, an emphasis was placed on the relationship between ethnic identity and political rights, mixed with the need to redress the wrongs of the past into new definitions of local territorial dominion based on the ethnic-historic presence of the largest local population (in Panchthar, the Limbu people).

73 The lesson plan included seven interactive sections: 1) Cold peace *vs.* warm peace – the feeling of security, social harmony, trust, a heart free from fear, cooperation among people; 2) Expressions of social violence (obvious and hidden); 3) What to do?; 4) Causes of lack of peace (social, environmental, economic, psychological, structural); 5) Development after a civil war; 6) SZOP; and 7) Peace Town.

In the name of identity politics, the insurgency gained in emotional force and willing foot soldiers. Long after the signing of the Peace Agreement, awareness of a local sense of time and place and its significance for the evolution of the populace continue to impregnate provincial politics. The government and influential bodies of civil society initiated the institutionalized expression of this consciousness via the revival of local languages and the embedding of a "local curriculum" in national school education, especially for the elementary level. To date, however, the local curriculum is not mandatory. It is up to the schools to implement it for pupils who have difficulty in learning in Nepali if their parents communicate in Limbu only. Mr. Lawati, himself a Limbu, has designed a curriculum on local natural resources.

A very simple survey was suggested for older students to conduct by themselves with their peers, their parents and their teachers. They were free to change the questions as they saw fit, which they did not.

In 2013, the respondent group turned out to be rather small and can be treated as a sample: 29 students, 18 parents and 12 teachers returned their filled-in surveys. Some selected results gave the following information:

To the statement "I observe that the school is a peaceful place," parents responded:

Not at all: 0

Seldom: 2

Sometimes: 3

Often: 4

Always: 7

It was suggested that this positive result be shared at the next parents' meeting. A discussion would be started as to how parents and teachers together may continue to raise the peacefulness of the school environment, as in demonstrating similar educational principles at home as in school.

To the statement "Boys tend to harass girls," teachers responded:

Not at all: 1

Seldom: 4

Sometimes: 5

Often: 2

Much too often: 0

The same statement, however, elicited the following response from the students:

Not at all: 2

Seldom: 4

Sometimes: 6

Often: 9

Much too often: 5

This difference shows the need for teachers to become more aware of the actual experience of pupils in the school environment. It should be discussed in teachers' meetings and how codes of conduct may guide children to develop mutual gender respect in their lives. Gender biases in teachers' behaviors are to be openly discussed, too. A healthy equilibrium between gender sensitivity and gender equity at school is difficult to attain and to maintain, and teachers should devote part of their weekly discussions to psychological and social issues that are so fundamental for the individual success of their female and male students – and for a peaceful society.

Teachers responded to the enquiry "When there is lack of peace at school, I think the causes are. . . ":

– Students' destructive behavior/state of mind
– Lack of moral education
– Home environment
– Need for more flexibility from school administration
– National situation of our country Nepal

These may be the starting points for regular school meetings among stakeholders to raise consciousness and develop strategies to address these issues constructively together.

General results from 2013 indicated that, on the whole, the school environment was perceived as peaceful. From 1 (low) to 5 (high), students gave an aggregated score of 3.8 to the question: "After a fight, teachers explain to students how to solve problems at school so that students learn appropriate behavior and conflict resolution." Teachers gave an aggregated score of 4.2 to the question: "As a teacher, I am happy to come to school. I feel included in the teachers' community and useful for the students' future." Parents gave an aggregated score of 4.1 to the question: "I notice that my child is receiving explicit peace education at school, through the topics taught."

In 2014, the respondent group was composed of 29 students, 17 parents, 13 teachers and 3 members of the school management committee, including the school principal.

The *teachers'* surveys showed the following perceptions:

- ANOVA testing giving a $p$ value of 0.34 revealed that "boys harassing girls" had decreased over the year to a statistically significant degree.[74]
- Teachers were observing fights at school to the same degree but were intervening and guiding conflict resolution more often.
- They felt more included in the teachers' community.
- They taught about peace more often in their curriculum subjects.
- They addressed the causes of lack of peace at school less often (whether this is due to less lack of peace or to less open discussion cannot be known here).
- Their own conflict management skills had remained the same as in 2013.

Samples of answers to "Causes for lack of peace at school" were: a) feelings of humiliation; b) impact of political affairs/instability of country; c) communication gap.

The *parents'* surveys showed the following perceptions:

- ANOVA testing giving a $p$ value of 0.006 revealed that "My child tells me of unhappy experiences at school" had decreased over the year to a statistically significant degree.

[74] In contrasting the questionnaire results from 2013 with those of 2014, the ANOVA (analysis of variance) statistical test was used in order to compare means from multiple groups. Obviously, there were various factors besides the peace education actions that could influence the results of the year-on-year surveys. An ANOVA test allows us to determine if the means between two groups are significantly different or not. That is to say, it allows us to eliminate the null-hypothesis, that all treatments or no treatment yield the same result.

- A small increase was noticeable in: a) perceiving the school as a peaceful place; b) actively cooperating in the civic and moral education of their children in alignment with the school's efforts.
- A small decrease was noticeable in: a) their children reporting happy experiences at school; b) their awareness of the peace topic being explicitly taught in class; c) supporting their children's homework.

Samples of answers to "For me, peace at school means…" were: a) students' unity; b) no quarrelling and no interference from political parties; c) respecting elders, teachers, brothers and sisters.

The*students'* surveys showed the following perceptions:

- ANOVA testing giving a p value of 0.004 revealed that "boys harassing girls" dropped appreciably.
- An increase was noticeable in: a) teachers stopping fights and explaining better ways to deal with conflict; feeling happy at school and included in the school community; observing peace and friendships; trusting that teachers will understand them.
- A decrease was noticeable in: a) fighting at school. A small decrease showed in the explicit teaching of the topic of peace by teachers in their classes.

Samples of students answers to "For me, peace at school means…" were: a) students' respect for teachers and teachers helping students solve their problems; b) not breaking rules or violating regulations in schools and other places; c) availability of good reading, learning and living environment.

The School Management Committee (SMC) including the headmaster said that sustainable peace at school required: a) giving good treatment to others and expecting good treatment from others; b) securing cooperation in order to face difficulties on the way to peace; c) contributing to surmounting difficulties by helping others and encouraging people to help one another.

Over the course of three years, the teachers' body and school management were requested to monitor and record particular aspects of school life in order to facilitate a qualitative evaluation afterwards. Suggested areas of observation were:

- Number of fights in the schoolyard
- Incidents of inappropriate behavior
- Aggregate number of hours teaching elements of a peace curriculum (social studies and other subjects)
- Number of occasional inclusions of peace topics in various disciplines

- Number of inclusions of peace topics in the local curriculum
- Meetings between teachers to talk about peace at school
- Meetings with parents to talk about peace at school
- Other quantitative and qualitative criteria to be selected by the stakeholders

Such long-term observation of some peace dimensions in school life and the regular recording of pre-defined criteria proved difficult to sustain. This does not exclude, however, the possibility of repeating the experiment and engaging all the stakeholders in a deepened social experiment. Students of social sciences and education may be interested in furthering such observational studies.

During this period, I had the opportunity to meet with three different District Education Officers. They all were kind and helpful and always provided me with the data I requested. The DEO of the years 2014–15 stands closer to the study in the sense that he considered it his core mission to declare all schools of Panchthar Zones of Peace. Three years after the policy declaration by the government, this concept and practice had finally entered the region – and powerfully so.

During a previous conversation with the Director General of the Education Department and Chairman of the National Committee of SZOP, Dr. Lava Awasthi, he had pointed out that "first, we had to protect the children from harm during the conflict, then we had to ensure their undisturbed attendance at school in the immediate post-conflict events, now we need to create a culture of peace at the heart of schools." This was central to the agenda of Mr. Gyan Mani Nepal, then DEO of Panchthar, who said: "All districts are declared SZOP and children attend school no matter the political events surrounding them. I have the support of all the leaders now."

The educational officer pointed out that SZOP is not just about keeping schools open in case of strikes, it is a commitment by SMCs, guardians, teachers, older students and groups external to schools to refrain from any kind of political intervention or ideological politicization. SZOP is the national mandate to implement the Rights of the Child in each school of the country by creating a child-friendly environment and eradicating detrimental behaviors such as sexual harassment or corruption within school-related proccsses.

A law enacted in 2000 stipulates that schools must open 220 days of the year, but research then showed that in Panchthar, during the few years after the insurgency, they had only been open an average of 79 days. Since then, teachers' strikes over political demands and problems such as absenteeism or drunkenness at school were punished, and good civil service towards the education of children was rewarded. Teachers' training increased and solid management of schools, curriculum, tests and exams took place. Importantly, Mr. Nepal received the commitment of parents, teachers, principals and political groups to turn all schools of Panchthar into Zones of Peace. There may have been broken promises at first, yet at the time of our first interview in 2014, Mr. Nepal affirmed positive developments. In the campaigning for SZOP in Panchthar, over 1,000 people – students, teacher and parents – had signed for peace. The leaders of political parties expressed their support (not at first, but as they saw that the people supported it, then they did so too). Members of Parliament also explicitly support the policy, he affirmed.

Today, one can observe ease and friendship in the school yard of the SPHSS. As the psycho-social environment increasingly sustains its peaceability, it is the class management of students' intellectual and cognitive capacities through varied teaching methods that becomes the next priority. SPHSS is intent on achieving higher scores on School-Leaving Certificate (SLC) examinations year-on-year and ensuring a peaceful environment that enables this.

In May 2015, we conducted an interaction with Mr. Bhandari, Mr. Lawati, teachers, older students, parents and members of the school management committee as well as the DEO, Mr. Nepal. Reflecting on the simple yet relevant quantitative results of the previous two years, we were glad to conclude that an overall peaceability increase at the school was a shared experience among the stakeholders. Before parting, we agreed to sustain and deepen this peace by following a three-fold path:

1. *Include references to peace concepts and peace examples in curriculum-centered and extra-curricular lessons* regularly (teachers will initiate creative applications in the subjects taught).
2. *Teach in a peaceful way*, with attitudinal and behavioural expressions of respect, equal treatment and encouragement of students, colleagues and guardians. This entails continued application and propagation of the policy of Schools as Zones of Peace as proclaimed by the Government of Nepal in 2011.
3. *Seek examples in Nepal and in the world that exemplify social equity,*

*good governance and sustainable economic development, and base the management and daily life of the school on these precepts* (the school becomes a center of learning for the community as opposed to a closed system for the sole purpose of sitting exams).

## 2. Mechi English Boarding School (Case Study 2)

The Phidim Gadi is a hill of some 200 meters overlooking Phidim's town center. It was once the site of a Limbu fort to plan warfare and also to make peace treaties and worship. There we find a temple, the statue of spiritual leader Phalgunanda, a community radio station, a school and two shops providing students with sweets and drinks. The Limbu temple is in the open air, with majestic trees, meaningful stones, colorful banners and all sizes of bells to attract the Gods' attention to the devotees' prayers. Two hours away from Phidim is the Prangbung Gadi, once used by Limbus to fight against the Gurkhas or other Kirats in periods of clan belligerence. Further still is the Yangnam Gadi. And so a long chain of high hilltops filled with Limbu ancestry.

History records that long ago, when 10 Limbu tribes had long been quarrelling, they finally united at the Phidim Gadi by performing the "ceremony of promise." The clan chiefs, aided by spiritual guides, combined their statement of peacemaking with symbolic gestures involving soil, grass, water and stones. Nature – the omnipresent environment for protection and livelihood – was the witness of their reconciliation. The Phidim Gadi hence has been anchored as a place of reunion, compromise and reconciliation – all components of peacemaking.[75]

### *The Selling Family*

Adjacent to the temple is the Mechi English Boarding School. The temple foliage gives shade to the schoolyard and Phalgunanda seems to bless each junior generation with intellectual and moral awakening. The school was

[75] It was in 2010, when standing on the Phidim Gadi next to Phalgunanda, that I decided to engage in a study of peace education at the heart of the Limbu land, aware it would take repeated visits over several years.

first established as a primary school in 1983 by a Limbu man, Nuresh Selling, after returning from Darjeeling, India. He founded a family in Phidim with his wife Sita and they had three children. After some years, the school expanded to the secondary level, until class X. A visionary educationalist, Mr. Selling was leading a respectable establishment when he and his daughter died in a motorcycle accident. Sita Selling raised the two younger sons on her own and stepped into the role of school principal.

Madam Sita is a Limbu personality, an incarnation of local spirit. She is often clad in white, the Limbu traditional colour and that of age, maturity or wisdom in South Asia (also of mourning in the Hindu tradition). Sita has traversed difficult situations that have made her a rock of faith. She has found strength in cultural spirituality to survive existential challenges.

Throughout the years, while some parents were able to pay the school fees and boarding costs, many others left their children in the caring hands of the Mechi English Boarding School, unable to contribute financially. Children were never sent away for financial reasons. One of the most dramatic periods was during the Maoist insurgency when partisans came up to the school to demand "donations" (money, food). Sita had to hand out goods for fear of reprisals, yet most times she managed to make the Maoist rebels aware that the children's needs were greater than their own. She was equally put to the test by the opposite fighting party: the Phidim police department, situated at the bottom of the hill, was vulnerable to insurgents' attacks and ordered her to let her school become their headquarters so as to fight the Maoists better from the hilltop. Sita held her ground to stop this from happening.

Sita does not speak English (as the teachers and students do), nor does she have knowledge about curriculum, didactics or world affairs, but she is the mast and the wheel of the school. Her management style has been typical of a one-woman, crises-steady, value-driven and control-based leadership. In recent years, however, and also in line with our experiment, an increasingly team-based management has been developing in the school – also as a consequence of the peace program.

Symbolic of a center of learning deeply rooted in local culture, the Mechi School houses a small *manghim* (Limbu for "mandir" or temple). It feels like the whole school has a spiritual character, anchoring its mission each day to combine international English, intellectual and technical effort, and a yearning for modernity yet with a timeless consciousness of place.

In 2014, the school had 750 students, 30 of whom were boarding. All 33 students of class X passed their SLC exam that year, making Mechi the only school in Panchthar with 100% SLC success.

## *Action Research at Mechi*

For the period between 2011 and 2014, the school agreed to participate in an experiment to deepen the reality of peace in the day-to-day lives of the students, teachers and parents. It was agreed that each teacher, on a regular basis, would link his or her subject (biology, mathematics, chemistry, Nepali, etc.) with the notion of peace and offer concrete examples of how peace may be linked with the subject.

The creative implementation was left to the teachers to do as each saw fit. While the first year showed much enthusiasm during my presence, it fell into oblivion while I was in Europe. The second year had greater momentum and the third year saw a definite operationalization of the peace strategy in all school matters, also during my absence.

The plan was twofold: 1) teach about peace; and 2) teach peacefully. Both – content and context – would engender a cultural demonstration of peace as a driver at the heart of the educational establishment. This would enable a passage from the residues of war (in children and adults' imaginations, repressed traumas or leftover communication styles of enmity) to peaceful ways.

### Teaching about Peace

The teachers agreed to include references to peace, whatever their subjects. When preparing their teaching plans, they would make a point to include at least one reference to peace in each lesson. For example, they could measure the bows of temples dedicated to the Lord Buddha in geometry; in biology, they would demonstrate how microscopic amoeba, as much as large animals, both compete and cooperate for territory and evolution; in history, they would study the peace processes that followed wars and insurgencies; in English, they would read the lives of peacemakers; in Nepali, they would write poems about the search for peace in the human heart; in social science, they would study the development of a country towards social equity; in political science, they would learn about national and international systems that aim to secure peace; in environmental studies, about the re-lationships between human settlements and industries and their impact on sustainability; the local curriculum would focus on cultures of peace in the lives and rituals of ancestors.

The teachers committed themselves to this disciplined approach of preparing and imparting lessons. During each of my yearly visits, I also taught lessons at the Mechi School (classes IX and X) – on the meaning, expression and necessity of peace, confirming the teacher-led experiment that was happening in their school. Everyone was on the same page.

### Teaching Peacefully

The teachers agreed to engage in a cultural experiment. By way of their own attitude and behavior while teaching, they would aim to uplift the school environment and make it a place where parents and visitors would experience its peacefulness. By dedicating itself to peace education, the school endorsed teaching styles that felt peaceful.

It was agreed to refrain from using the stick if discipline or punishment were necessary. Instead, the teachers would take time to find a clear and respectful communication that appealed to the conscience of the child. Their metaphor was to put the stick up on the wall as a feature in a museum, to be referred to for its former use. The teachers agreed not to slap, shout or be angry with the students. They expressed the desire to have good and interesting relationships with the parents. They particularly valued their role in teaching subjects well, so that students pass with distinction and succeed later in life in intelligent and useful activities.

The teachers agreed to work on themselves as people and become more peaceful individuals, so as to "walk the talk." Since they had some areas of conflict (with the school management, with particular students or with some parents), we discussed these issues and explored how to solve them successfully. This required the courage to explain a given situation, to stay true to one's feelings about it and to make an appeal for change in a respectful, clear and open manner. Over time, the teachers commented on the improvement of all previous difficult relationships. Madam Sita's own learning curve included some release of personal authority into the capable hands of her team of teachers so that a more democratic style of management could unfold in the Mechi School. By releasing some managerial tasks, she now sees herself free to write and teach a local cultural and spiritual curriculum to small children, which will be a strong foundation for their future personalities.

Each year, we discussed the implementation of "peace rules" with the students. By 2014, classes IX and X had created their own "class constitutions" based on fundamental peace tenets and articles of "dos" and "don'ts." It was an exercise of consultation, democracy, consensus and passing of classroom laws for all to abide by. As a process facilitated by the teachers, the constitutions were written by the students and hung by the entrance door. It included peaceful measures of redress in the form of non-harmful punishment if a student ignored a rule of the constitution out of bad will or carelessness. The measure or degree of punishment was defined by the students collectively at the onset. The internal peace program would be explicitly mentioned in the end-of-year celebration and during open days. Of course, this process would have to be renewed each year in order to enter deeper cultural levels of school life.

Examples of rules written by the pupils to be applied by themselves and by teachers, parents and the school management:

1. Students will respect teachers because teachers give knowledge and want the best for the students.
2. Teachers will respect students because students are individuals that will continue to build the nation.
3. Respect is shown in polite manners, from both teachers and students: there is no abuse, humiliation, ridicule, discrimination or arrogance.
4. Classes start and finish on time so that time is a well-managed resource.
5. The seating arrangement changes every month so as to create strong yet flexible communities.
6. There are two class managers (girl and boy) for queries of a practical and social nature. These students are elected for six-month periods. They are responsible for delegating tasks equitably to other students over time, such as cleanliness of the class, fetching materials, preparation of events, etc.
7. There are two teachers (female and male) to whom students can go for any matters.

8. If a student has a question, s/he raises her/his hand and waits to be addressed.
9. When teacher-centered, the class will not be disturbed by students talking.
10. When student-centered, the class will participate actively and students will communicate when asked.
11. The level of noise will be consciously kept low.
12. If one or more students are purposely or carelessly disturbing the class, they will leave the class until they agree to observe the rules.
13. Punishment may include: cleaning, helping management with administrative tasks, helping younger children with their school work, helping in the kitchen after school hours.

### Value-driven Establishment

Ethical values were discussed with both teachers and students in meetings and classroom interactions, in particular on the topics of obedience, discipline and the building of personality. To exemplify community and union, we highlighted "sameness" through school uniforms, classroom constitutions, establishment rules and a common curriculum for the same tests and exams. Obedience and discipline are values which, when anchored in behavior, contribute to order and equity, strengthening equivalency, playing down differences and preventing the abuse of individuals or groups over others. Yet obedience can also be wrongly channeled if it becomes blind following. After all, it takes obedient people to execute the bad will of despots or to fulfill orders without understanding their purpose. So obedience for its own sake can be fully devoid of responsibility or morality.

An individual conscience, on the other hand, questions whether a particular discipline really helps attain the common good. This conscience is a decision-maker, an arbiter of what is to be obeyed or not, and the reasoning behind this difference. A peace teacher encourages obedience to the degree that it awakens free will in the student. Self-discipline then becomes like an engine for the student who feels the power of his or her own choice of action in doing good. This is at the heart of peace pedagogy.

Interaction

In the course of yearly interactions, together we defined tolerance, respect, kindness and truth. The teachers expressed their difficulties with carelessness and impoliteness on the part of the students, and discussed how a culture of peace could redress some behaviors for the better. In 2014, there was a celebration of our peace research and a meeting with parents, followed by a day of teachers' training. For the final year of the experiment, teachers agreed to some small but significant things:

1. Eradicate the terms "I can't" (for themselves and with their students).
2. Increase self-confidence and awareness of one's contribution to the Mechi School ("This is the gift I bring. . . ").
3. Use regularly the technique of Active Listening with all stakeholders.
4. Perform conflict management (prevention, resolution, lessons learned) whenever possible.

Already in the course of the first two years, teachers said they had noticed a change in the school life and expressed gladness for the experiment. They commented that the students themselves had decided they should remain silent when their teacher speaks. In comparison to previous years, classes had become a lot quieter.

Micro-teaching was on the increase, which helped teachers build deeper relationships with each of their students. The notion of peace was shared little by little, child by child. There was a keener sense of time management, applying better methods to keep the children interested and busy, curbing idleness, learning to use time properly.

A female Limbu mathematics teacher said that she had used the stick often in the previous years but now had become ashamed of her teaching style. She sought to be more peaceful herself to demonstrate a behavior that children would want to copy.

A male maths teacher explained: "I told them a story which I wrote myself, because I publish stories." It tells of a man who gets ill (the person is a metaphor for Nepal). Seeking help to recover his health, he goes to see the best doctor in the country, Dr. Bhagwan. The doctor suggests several treatments and observes the effects of traditional as well as the newest medicine on his patient. Unfortunately, the illness does not recede and the man gets more and more ill over time. The doctor, concerned about his patient and sorry about his inability to help, decides to withdraw from practice in order to search for a more appropriate, more effective cure. Now free from his busy schedule, he starts an intensive medical and psychological experiment with the patient. Each day, he tells him false or exaggerated news about how much corruption is growing in the country. Over a short period of time, the man's health gets worse and worse and he soon becomes so weak he might die. Then, the doctor reverses the experiment and tells his patient that corruption has stopped and people are handling all matters of life together in a fair and transparent way, with the removal of barriers against opportunities for all. Over time, the patient gets better, and by hearing stories of the end of corruption, the ailments leave his body. The doctor's scientific experiment and dedication towards this unique patient leads to understanding healing and preventive health.

"The students loved the story; they understood deeply," says the maths teacher. "I cannot afford to tell stories often because the maths program is so full, but such story-telling helps build the relationship between the class and the teacher; it deepens their curiosity and listening skills."

### Results

The atmosphere between students has deepened in positivity, and adult-centered conflicts are being resolved in an increasingly open dialogue. All say that they have benefited from this injection of peace awareness. When asked about the new frontier of peacemaking, Ms. Selling speaks of her concern at seeing some young citizens in the municipality ruin their minds, their health and their future (and that of Nepal) by consuming much alcohol in town and living idle lives. A school as a Zone of Peace may counteract early tendencies within its walls; the next level, however, would be served by establishing a "Town as Zone of Peace." This lies within the parameters of good governance and the creation of opportunity, which are on the agenda of future (long-awaited) democratically elected local governments.

## 3. Alternative Energy Development Centre Nepal (Case Study 3)

Panchthar district was deeply touched by the Maoist insurgency (especially the last six years of its 10-year duration). Study interviews have reflected the opinion that the actions of insurgents created more pain than relief. Development progress was halted, economic infrastructures were demolished,

Village Development Committee (VDC) offices and other government/non-government offices were ransacked, records were burnt, rules and regulations were discarded. One generation missed out on education. Many households had to migrate, and the homeless could not get enough humanitarian help or human rights protection. Every aspect of life was severely threatened, in every town, village and community (socio-economic ties, food security, school attendance, health, communication, development).[76]

Local NGOs are grassroots structures of civil society that have played an important role as peaceful social transformers in the transition phase since 2006 and before that. Panchthar counts some 500 registered NGOs, a tenth of which are actively involved in social development design. Immediately after the CPA, most NGOs focused on informal education about basic rights (human rights, citizens' rights, women's rights, children's rights, etc.) and the peace process at the community level (reintegration of Maoists, return of property, allowances, working with the peace agenda). Often in collaboration with the Local Peace Committees (LPCs), NGOs ran programs to raise awareness about health, gender equality, citizens' rights and duties, and the rule of law. Women's groups, citizens' groups and community mobilizers prepared the way for peace by addressing needs for social equality, economic solidarity, informal education, village infrastructure development, and post-conflict reconciliation and healing.

AEDC is a case in point with its multi-disciplinary, practical implementation of societal development through technologies appropriate for the region.

---

76 This account does not reflect the opinion of the author who was not in Nepal during that time, who generally studies the ubiquity of insurgencies at all times across the world, and generally aims to refrain from judgment. Undeniably, the insurgency also brought radical changes. The causes presented by the Maoists as to their motive for going to war against the government were later taken as the new national agenda. Awareness-raising efforts regarding equality, equal distribution of opportunities, the need for behavioral change across social groups and an increase of participation by civil society became potent features of Nepal's politics. The UN, the international community and the Nepali nation as a whole became closer partners and mutually accountable solution-seekers for the eradication of poverty within a short period of time. Social and political groups approached these issues with various degrees of radicalization, which caused yet more years of disputes in parliamentary chambers and on the streets. Even if sometimes it has felt much like treading water, Nepal, nonetheless, has surely been on the move towards improvement.

### *AEDC*

Dependent on donors' funding, this NGO bids to execute projects that answer local needs. It runs projects like the construction of micro-hydro power plants, the installation of sanitary facilities district-wide ("one home, one toilet") or perennial programs such as informal education of good governance. AEDC's initial mission is to sponsor appropriate, renewable technology in order to facilitate community self-reliance.

Acting as a catalyst for local self-help solutions to address rural development challenges and prevent environmental degradation, AEDC facilitates initiatives in income generation activities (IGAs), sustainable development planning and community-based natural resource management. Supportive of good governance through decentralization, the NGO works with civic institutions, communities and government to improve access to public services, to mainstream public participation in development reform and to promote the integration of local priorities in development policy.[77]

### *Cooperation between AEDC and the Peace Study*

AEDC expressed its interest in supporting the action research. The board and the members agreed that all alternative energy and livelihood projects between 2012 and 2015 would explicitly make a direct link to peace. After several meetings with all staff, AEDC ensured that it would clearly, publicly and continuously connect the good governance element of their projects to the contribution this brings to societal peace. Every project would ensure that each communication with stakeholders and beneficiaries exemplifies

[77] The Poverty Alleviation Fund (PAF) is one such long-term program funded by the World Bank. The Phidim Second Small Town Water Supply Sanitation Sector Project is 50% funded by the ADB, the rest by the Nepali government and 5% by consumers. The biomass energy project in all VDCs of Panchthar is funded by the government of Nepal and the Alternative Energy Promotion Centre (AEPC). The improved watermill program in all VDCs of Panchthar (also taking place in the districts of Taplejung and Terathum) is funded by the government of Nepal and AEPC. Government funds are usually understood as mixed bundles from more than seven donors whose monies are channeled under selected priorities within the government's five-year development plan. At the time of writing, three VDCs have been covered, one of which is Siwa. All projects involve putting infrastructure systems in place at village level, training users, strengthening community policy-level decisions, operation of local systems, monitoring and evaluation.

the contribution to peace by implementing the principles of good governance (transparency, accountability, participation). This linkage would be a conscious, shared educational driver throughout all activities.

AEDC is a reliable partner for 23 community-based organizations (CBOs) to date, all of which are involved in self-help/mutual activities such as vegetable-growing, the production of ginger or the keeping of goats and pigs. The social mobilizers go there to support, train and check that everything happens according to the principles of good governance and whole-family support (keeping books, decision-making, purchasing and selling, redistributing earnings, encouraging, etc.): this is an element of democracy through self-help at grassroots level. The social mobilizers were instructed to explicitly link their work to peace with every single program and in their training.

Community development works at least in two ways: 1) how fairly and positively the community organizes itself within an open societal structure, clarifying its needs and engaging people in their realization; and 2) how responsive higher level (structurally empowering) institutions are to the development needs of these communities. The quality of livelihood grows from the quality of decisions that communities make over a long period of time and the mutual influence with higher levels of district administration. Both bottom-up and top-down approaches are necessary, and AEDC, as any local NGO, often has the role of interface between the two.[78] The following example of Siwa VDC illustrates a case of socio-economic development related to good governance and peace.

[78] To assess remote communities in Nepal, field studies make use of the Participatory Rural Appraisal (PRA) and Appreciative Enquiry (AI) methods. These help to find out all about the people's lives, occupations, earnings, sources of fuel, activities, feelings, etc. Consultative meetings are also held with VDC secretaries and DDC officials at the district level at the onset of the studies. Simple statistical tools enable measurement criteria. Qualitative data is analyzed, transcribed and interpreted into descriptive writing. The core situation assessment (CSA) tool was developed by United Mission to Nepal (UMN). It helps to understand baseline measurement in a community, identify potential target communities and working areas and helps in the planning and evaluation of initial and ongoing programs. It has a 0–1 index (0 is a good situation, 1 is a poor situation).

### *Profile of Siwa*

In 2015, Siwa became part of the municipality and now comprises wards IX, X and XI of the Phidim town. At the time of our study, it was a VDC of its own with nine wards. Reachable from Phidim on foot within two hours, it is also connected via a track road for vehicles. Due to their remoteness, the inhabitants of Siwa had a lower socioeconomic status in comparison with other groups in the area. Various agencies sought to help lift their living standard, in line with the broader strategy of Nepal meeting the Millennium Development Goals. As part of the country-wide development objectives, the Nepal Red Cross Society worked in water, sanitation and hygiene projects (externally-funded) in Siwa. The Poverty Alleviation Fund (PAF) worked in empowerment and the improvement of livelihoods. Importantly, Siwa did not have electricity.

Siwa counted 714 households and an average household size of six people at the time of the Social Impact Study (SIS) in 2011. Of these households, 25% were selected at random for primary data through survey interviews with key informants (*e.g.*, heads of families) and field observations. Secondary data was collected from government offices and other agencies. Only four households of the 178 surveyed did not own the house they were living in. Of the population, 94.79% had access to safe drinking water in the community (private taps for the majority of households, community taps/wells for a few). Single remote home-dwellers had to walk long distances to fetch water in the village.

To understand the full situation of the Siwa VDC, consultations were arranged with other organizations: the DDC office, Alternative Energy Promotion Center (AEPC), Energy Support Assistance Program (ESAP), the National Planning Commission, the Water and Energy Commission Secretariats (WECS), and the association of small and cottage industries, FECOFUN.

The last census (2011) reported religious affiliations as 67% Kirat, 24% Buddhist, 7% Hindu, 1% Christian, 1% other and 0% Islam. Siwa seemed one of the most Limbu-populated concentrations in Panchthar (53%), although the then wards 3 and 4 had a majority of Magars. Brahmin and Chhetri were spread through all the wards, yet comparatively fewer in relation to other social groups.

Siwa displayed a high level of school drop-outs, few SLCs and about

20% of the population was illiterate. The people there are either working in agriculture or are young pupils. Many men go abroad for jobs, yet return before 50 years of age to continue their work in agriculture. Migration occurs easily (Limbus seem to migrate readily, both within Nepal and abroad).

### *Good Governance and Peace in Siwa with AEDC*

In 2007, Debendra Basnet, a water expert, was walking from village to village. When he reached Siwa, he spoke about the potential of the nearby river for a micro-hydro plant to produce electricity for Ward 7 and beyond.[79]

Under his guidance, a committee was formed to write a proposal and present it to NCDC Ilam (an NGO in alternative technology promotion). NCDC forwarded this proposal to AEDC, as Siwa is situated in Panchthar (the two NGOs share a history of cooperation in local energy projects). In turn, AEDC handed it over to the village committee. The Maluwa Siwa Khola Micro Hydro User Committee was formed and registered at the District Development Committee of Panchthar as per the Water Use Act, with a chairman, vice-chairman, secretary, co-secretary, treasurer and members.

The Multipower Construction Company Pvt. Ltd. (from Kathmandu) was selected for the works. The inhabitants helped with the construction (planting poles, carrying stones, digging, laying pipes to homes). The DDC provided 50 wood poles. Each house contributed 80 kg of pebbles and eight 50-kg sacks of sand. From canalization works starting in 2008 to full completion in 2010, the project of electrification had taken only two years. This successful event received much attention in the local and national media. It was a collective work that affirmed citizens' leadership for positive change, equality, teamwork, good governance and the common sharing of results.

The VDC of Siwa financed the project with 750,000.00 NPR and the DDC of Panchthar with 30,000 NPR as grants. The national government's Ministry of Science and Technology gave 467,500 NPR as a subsidy through the government's subsidy delivery mechanism.

A deal was made with each household to purchase a minimum of 25 watts. As an initial investment, 85 households bought 25 watts for 3,600 NPR in advance, as an estimation of their future use. Some households knew they would use more, so they bought 125 watts. One watt cost 144

[79] In 2013, Ward 7 counted 85 households (largely composed of Tumruk families) with on average 5 people per household.

NPR. The capacity of each household according to this payment deal was registered on the household's power meter. If a household used more electricity, it would pay more accordingly. The capacity of the river is 5.5 kilowatts in the dry season. In the rainy season, it rises to 10 kilowatts. In 2013, a household's usage was about 125–150 watts. This gave an availability of 12 hours per day on average, as required by the households.[80]

Our research visits occurred in 2011 (at the celebration of the first anniversary of the micro-hydro plant) and in 2013 (the second visit was to strengthen data and conclude observations).

The example of Siwa shows that any village near a river with a sufficient gradient can harness electricity in this way. It demonstrates that good coordination in the project works: its financing, upkeep and maintenance are all possible through good organization and good spirit. It points to the role of NGOs in alternative technology and to their importance in the development of Nepal. It exemplifies how good governance at local level (clear financial data, democratic involvement, an elected representative committee, fair and equitable distribution of the resource) is a means of empowerment, of development and of societal stability. The project's initial investment had occurred through funders and the inhabitants' financial and labor participation. It had taken two years to be operational. The legal process had occurred in compliance within the Nepal Electricity Policy of the government.

### *Applied Correlation between Good Governance and Peace*

In this section, we attempt to link some elements of GG at the heart of the Siwa case study with the existence and anchoring of peace.

---

80 The daily use does not allow for kitchen equipment such as refrigerators, only for a few water boilers. There are no washing machines. About 70% of the households have TV, 100% have radio (also using solar cells). There are no computers (only two in the school) and no individual laptops (yet). The light has helped the children do their homework in the evening, an advantage for learning. Yet the electricity is not sufficient to be used in farming or other food-based production and business. The village is now asking for an expansion of their plant to enable them such an upgrade into business-oriented economic development.

### Legal Framework and Democratic Process

There is a constitution or written framework that sets the purpose, policies, rules and regulations of the hydro-plant for the benefit of all villagers. This was part of the registration and did not require any alteration over the following years. There is a board or committee that oversees the alignment between electricity-making and distribution to households, in concordance with the constitution. This committee meets every three months. The members are selected for one-year periods, after discussion – or, in case of disagreement, after voting. If an important point must be discussed, villagers are requested to assemble. All users have understood and have agreed to the by-laws that are the basic rules for the users' group.

### Transparency

The legal body overseeing this infrastructure is a committee comprised of 15 people. They select the members of the board. This selection is agreed by the village. The books show the operator's monthly salary, which is 4,200 NPR. After paying all expenses, an average of 1,600 NPR is collected monthly into a fund for the future expansion of power generating capacity. External auditing occurs through the DDC each fiscal year, when the committee has to renew its existence. Household billing is done monthly, according to ward administration, and household consumption is visible via the meters. Any interested person may have access to the books.

### Accountability

Accountability derives from the previous two factors (democracy and transparency). Results are given by the representatives in a clearly understandable way. There is the possibility to address all questions related to the project by anyone at any time. The success of the project on a long-term basis also has a lasting impact on community trust as social capital.

### Conflict Regulation – Mediation System

In case of a problem, disagreement or conflict, a discussion or an internal mediation takes place. No matter the time it takes, it will end successfully with a solution for that difficulty (be it human or technical). The handling of community problems is a long-established capability in villages, and outright conflicts between inhabitants over shared resources seldom happen (maybe due to a common social base and the aspiration to never return to violent conflicts). If a problem were to arise, the inhabitants say that they would deal with it in a village-democratic fashion. In the case of a more complicated problem, they would follow the legal route (paralegal, police or court). When asked whether they feel free to bring up any question for an open discussion at the village level, the inhabitants unanimously answered "yes."

### Looking for the Peace Component in Siwa's Best Practice

Searching for the link between energy-making in a rural area, good governance and peace, we asked the people if they experienced peace in daily life and if that peace had grown since electrification. The inhabitants (two focus groups of about 20 people in 2011 and 2013 respectively) responded that they felt a greater sense of happiness – increased contentment – since having access to electricity, rather than "peace" as such. They also felt proud to have done it together in this way, satisfied at reaching their goal and getting exactly what they expected. They felt enabled and pleased to have fully understood and participated in the process. "Happy" would be a better choice of word, as compared to "peaceful."

What had also increased was a sense of community and trust in one another: "We can achieve things together, and so we can do more still. We believe in ourselves more." When asked about lack of peace, for example misunderstandings or disputes, the focus groups admitted to small quarrels but dismissed them as normal, small and trivial things that were not worth spending time on.

When asked whether *"economic peace" had increased due to the outcomes of electricity-making* (*e.g.*, more business, more comfortable life, economic upgrade), the inhabitants gave a negative answer: "We still have much to do. Electricity has not brought us more business. Indeed, we need more business, more income-generation activities. On our soil, we can grow anything for it is good earth, but we lack transportation means and direct connections to markets. There were middlemen who encouraged us in the past and bought our produce, but some were not honest and we lost farming business due to their malpractice. So now we are cautious and seeking new opportunities. We cannot say that electricity has provided answers at that level."

When asked whether access to TV channels would introduce more violence to peasant families and their children, and present a distorted (very seldom peaceful) view of the world, the Siwa people said they understood the concern in this question but still perceived watching TV as development, entertainment and access to information.

When inhabitants were asked if there was social equality in the village, they unanimously answered yes. Good governance? Yes. Sustainable economic development? No.

Maybe if there was sustainable economic development the word "peace" would gain in meaning in the respondents' minds. Perhaps economic peace is still unimaginable, as the happiness of creating energy would have been inconceivable to the Tumruks' grandparents. By missing market development opportunities, having a low sense of entrepreneurship and with high levels of school dropouts, economic peace will take longer to arrive.

Regarding gender equality as a criterion for peace, we could observe that the Tumruk (Limbu) women of Siwa felt stronger and more equal than many rural or urban women of other groups. The women we met seemed to stand strong in their natural female power and possessed a large sense of humor. However, they seldom took leading positions (in committees, for example) because, they said, they had too much domestic work to do. So this rural society continues to be led externally by men, even though psychological strength is obvious in Tumruk women as much as in Tumruk men.

## 4. The Peace Trail (Case Study 4)

A component of the planned study was the creation of a peace park.[81] This required cooperation with the Forestry Department of the Government of

[81] Peace parks have been established in many countries. Many are transboundary and thus answer to the definition of the Transboundary Protected Area Network as "areas that are formally dedicated to the protection and maintenance of biological diversity and of natural and associated cultural resources, and to the promotion of peace and cooperation" (Ali, 2007). They are often situated on territories adjoining two or three bordering countries that have had an armed conflict, as a statement of peace between them. They are also found inside countries that have gone through violent, internal strife and are symbols as havens of peace, open to all former disputants.

Nepal, at least at the local level. A peace park would be officially established in the district of Panchthar and this declaration would be linked to a longitudinal study of peace-related social data gathered by the researcher and the park's inhabitants themselves.

In 2011, I met with the representative of the Department of Forests for the district of Panchthar, in the Phidim office. The idea of a peace park was presented to him as "an ecological sphere where human settlement not only cares to protect the fauna and flora (which it already does) but is also consciously dedicated to peace in explicit ways of living with nature and with one another as people." Importantly, it was to be anchored as a grassroots participation in structural peace in the form of "living and learning together, caring for the environment and deriving economic stability, even growth, from these healthy correlations." The District Chief of Forestry (DCF) agreed to help and gave me indications as to where and with whom to start. A chart of actions related to SE, GG and SED would be explained to the inhabitants and monitored over several years. An evaluation of whether they genuinely experienced "more peace" would be conducted as a conclusion to the experiment. We decided on a special area of the district but, as the rainy season had just started, we had to postpone the working visit and actual start of the study to the following year.

When I returned in 2012, the idea of a peace park had moved up the hierarchy of the Forestry Department to the highest echelons of the Government of Nepal. When visiting the Forestry Office in Phidim, I was informed that the idea had now been taken up by the Ministry of Forests and Soil Conservation itself and the operational aspect had been entrusted to the hands of WWF-Nepal. I was very pleased that this was happening. In less than one year, a large cross-border peace park between India and Nepal across a region of the Himalayas (Taplejung district) was being conceptualized. The Joint Secretary of the ministry and his counterpart in Sikkim had put the new peace park, in the area of Kangchenjunga, on their talks agenda.

When visiting Taplejung that year, I talked with WWF and saw how pleased they were with the plan and how significant the project had become for them. Three points emerged for me in the necessary adaptation to this new situation:

1. There was no particular need for a peace park as a *transborder* project since India and Nepal had not had an armed conflict – one of the tra-

ditional circumstances giving rise to transborder peace parks. A shared ecological sphere would have sufficed. However, to dedicate this region to peace and to affirm Nepal and India as equal partners in this project is a beautiful and exemplary thing to do, and can only benefit everyone.

2. To declare an ecological and human area a Zone of Peace requires guidance as to how ways of living need to change in order to raise individual and collective consciousness, uplift socioeconomic realities (positive peace) and prevent regressions into violence, violations of rights or usurpation of power (negative peace). A matrix of different peace programs to accompany the statutory, ecological and social event should reinforce the meaning of the peace park on the very long-term. This would be installed for both the Nepali and Indian local populations, separately and together, at the grassroots and policy levels. Otherwise, the term "peace park" would have little impact in its true definition and purpose.
3. I now had to find another, a new – Nepal-only, Panchthar-only – potential area for a peace park. After all, the whole point of the study was to observe whether and how a peace program (schools, campus, radio, peace park, etc.) reduces the remnants of conflict in the transition phase. My geographic sampling was the specific region of the far-eastern hills of Panchthar that had suffered from intra-state conflict.

As I reiterated the purpose of a peace park not only as a study of social change but also its linkage to economic activities possibly related to peace tourism, the DCF suggested an alternative in the eastern part of the district. A remarkably beautiful area in the Chyangthapu VDC was being considered for development in tourism; why don't I visit and talk with his staff and the population there.

## *In Search of a Local Peace Park*

Hence, in May 2012, together with my local guide, assistant and interpreter Kulraj Subba, we travelled to Chyangthapu. The local representative of the Forestry Department (Mr. Tek Bahadur Chamling), the Chairman of Ward 3 (Mr. Bishweshor Begha), development staff, police officers, village dignitaries, school teachers and some interested youth had taken time to meet us. Kulraj explained the context of our initiative, the meaning of a peace park and the broad outline of the work involved in conducting an action research together.

The plan was to choose together an inhabited area in the district such as a ward, and, with the awareness, support and participation of the population, to discuss how to raise the experience and the standards of social equality, good governance and sustainable economic development by also expanding empathy, internal locus of control and basic trust at individual and household levels. The tasks would be attributed to three different commissions (SE, GG and SED) and the research methodology would provide them with survey sheets, measuring criteria and evaluation tools. Once a year I would visit to collect this information and reflect with everyone on the impact of the experiment.

Sitting in a circle in the open air, our group of hosts, some 12 people, had been listening attentively to Kulraj's translation, nodding with understanding and, seemingly, approval. One hour into the meeting, two gentlemen arrived with the loud knocking of a walking stick on the ground, a demonstrative laugh and a central positioning – first standing, then sitting – at the heart of the event, facing us in defiance. I had no idea what was going on.

This was not the time to demand explanations or insist on translations into English of what may be the matter with these two gentlemen. The rest of the group had become uneasy, silent, maybe confused or sorry for me ("the foreigner who has taken such pains to come all this way to visit them"). These are times when intercultural sensitivity, without knowledge of Nepali or Limbu language, is extremely limited and the Western need for immediate clarification, logical analysis and quick judgment should better be put on hold.

The two gentlemen were representatives of the Limbu people who believed in and propagated the establishment of an ethnic-based federal state of Limbuwan. My presence, made possible through cooperation with government representatives (foresters), was seen suspiciously as a collaboration with enemy principles – those of a pan-Nepal, state-administered, Kathmandu-power-centric, Brahmin-Chhettri-led, utilitarian-international-NGO-funded, externally-controlled governance of a land they considered ancestrally and contemporarily as "theirs." The presentation of the proposed action research in their local area had used some vocabulary that was of itself perceived as points of contention – in particular the term and notion of "community forests".

This is one of the many times when Kulraj showed his remarkable skills as representative and negotiator. He explained again and differently that the participative approach to studying SE, GG and SED could only be beneficial for all, that I did not favor any party nor carry any organization's agenda, that I was an independent peace scholar spending personal time and resources to understand Nepal better and modestly contribute to its peace process if I could (*i.e.*, being able to and enabled to). And for this to work, I needed their support. After 30 minutes, the large stick had stopped knocking on the ground and the provoking laughter had turned into dialogue.

The gentlemen voiced one clear condition to my freedom of movement and access to information and people in the area: I should not use the term "community forests" in my book. I understood why this was important to them and negotiated back that I should be able to use the term because as a researcher, I cannot ignore a 30-year old socioeconomic reality in the country. However, I would define the term without any partisanship to the particular framework of rural development that it advocates, and I would explain the deeply-rooted feelings and justifications behind their aversion against it. Thus it was agreed that a peace park may be considered and we had permission to go about and engage with our study.

The meeting concluded with the selection of a particular ward and area to start the work and individuals put themselves forward to be focus persons for the action research, to communicate locally about it and to collect data. Dimensions of study were explained and examples of actions were given. Five people volunteered to engage with good governance, social equality, economic development, environmental peace and spiritual peace, respectively. The group also said that unfortunately a Limbu leader, Mr. Machindra Begha, had not been able to attend the meeting yet was a key person for such decision-making and activities and that I should meet with him. The two gentlemen parted most amiably, giving us their mobile numbers and offering their help in any possible way.

That evening, we were invited to stay at Mr. Bishweshor Begha's home. Bishweshor was keen to support the study happening in his ward, shared much information, advocated for development through tourism and the construction of roads to raise economic activities through the sales of forestry products. He did not have any contention with any terminology.

## *A Peace Park as a Mitigating Factor*

Nepal's "Community Forestry"[82] program has been internationally acclaimed as a largely successful instrument for the socioeconomic development of rural areas. Started in the early 1980s, it has gone through various phases of deployment and operational focus.

In 2013, a comprehensive report on 30 years of community forestry in Nepal was published as an outcome of the Multi Stakeholder Forestry Programme (MSFP),[83] whose aim is to reduce rural poverty and increase resilience through the forestry sector. Important elements include the management of community-based forest resources, governance reform and participation, private sector involvement, and the mitigation of and adaptation to climate change.

Forests cover about 5.6 million hectares, roughly 40% of Nepal's territory (14.3 million ha). Of these forests, 23% are community forests – or 1.2 million ha – where 1.6 million households are organized and participate in 17,685 community forest user groups (CFUGs); this is about 33% of the total rural population. Forests are a significant productive resource amounting to 10% of GDP.[84]

The MSFP study was based on the social inclusion and sustainable livelihoods framework and captured change in three dimensions: 1) assets and services (natural capital, financial capital and physical capital); 2) voice and influence (social capital, human capital and political capital); and 3) rules of the game in terms of implementation of inclusive policies and institutions.

The Forest Act 1993 ensures the handing over of any parts of national forests to CFUGs for the purpose of conservation and collective utilization. A CFUG, if wanting to care for and use a forest area, must prepare

[82] With the Forest Act 1993, forests were divided into two categories of ownership: private and national. The latter are further subdivided into five attributes: 1) government-managed; 2) leasehold; 3) religious; 4) protected; and 5) community. Leasehold, religious and community forests are managed by user groups or local communities. Protected and government-managed forests are administered by government agencies. See Bhattarai (2014).

[83] The report, *Persistence and Change*, was the outcome of an independent study commissioned by the Ministry of Forests and Soil Conservation (MFSC) with support from the Swiss Agency for Development (SDC), the UK's Department for International Development (DFID) and Finland's Ministry for Foreign Affairs. Available at www.msfp.org.np.

[84] MFSC Department of Forests, 2011.

institutional rules for governance and develop a plan for management and exploitation in view of a fair distribution of tasks and rewards and in the framework of sustainable, ecological and economic development. Such a plan is prepared in consultation with the District Forest Office and is generally valid for 5 years after registration. The communities are allowed to harvest the benefits that accrue from such management, with prior agreement as to the apportioning for reinvestment or other local livelihood projects. The hours spent caring for the forests are distributed among the participating households and remunerated equally in cash. Ananda Bhattarai writes:

> In a nutshell, the community forest program reverses the hostile relationship created by the Forest Act of 1961 that derecognized the age-old [tenural] relation of local people with the forests and village commons in the neighbourhood. The new Act demonstrates how empowerment of the local people through recognition of their age-old use rights of common property resources creates motivation for their management and collective happiness.[85]

In view of the absence of elected local government since 1998, CFUGs have informally fulfilled many functions of local governance. They have provided an institutional space with clear and fair rules and processes, including a democratic way to make decisions.

The 2013 report by-and-large confirmed the positive aspects of community forests with aggregate increases of capital. Yet it also revealed that "deeply embedded cultural and behavioral practices that condition Nepali society remain within forest organizations and continue to be a significant barrier to change."[86] There was strong evidence of persisting patterns of social inequity (exclusion on the basis of caste, class, ethnicity, gender and household location). The ultra-poor continued to be extremely poor while the poor and middle class had been enjoying a rise in living standards as well as access to training and skill-enhancement. The richer class took up more of the forest management training and was also dominating in other functions such as chairmanships of VDCs, DDCs, etc. Local ethnic groups (Limbu, Rai) also had more access and voice in CFUG development.

Having a large community forest with several CFUGs and together making it experimentally into a Zone of Peace made complete sense to me. Where the CFUGs did well, we would draw from the learning of this

---

85 Bhattarai, *op. cit.*, 2.

86 MFSC, *Persistence and Change*, *op. cit.*, 5.

best practice to create a peace roadmap. Where the CFUGs did not do so well, we would apply the PACE Peaceability formula with intention and intensity over a couple of years and observe the results. Bishweshor Bhega supported this plan. When I left Nepal in July 2013, my hopes were with Mr. Bhega and the other volunteers who were going to communicate it to their communities and gather data against criteria.

When I returned in June 2014, forester Tek Chamling sought me out and with Kulraj's translation I was informed that the plan was on hold – entirely – and that I should meet with Limbu politician Machindra Begha. Of course, gladly. We traveled to Chyangthapu, Falaicha VDC, and were hosted by Machindra at his family home.[87] He was as keen to understand my purpose and my plan as I was to discover why the project had been suspended in my absence and what was motivating him as a Limbu politician. We spent many hours together, also reflecting upon the concept of "Limbuwan" he was advocating.

Sitting in the porch of his house, we talked of the purpose of a peace park. Machindra agreed with and accepted the objectives and proposed practices. There was nothing in the way. After being sure of my colors, he brought his official documents and maps to the table and spoke at length about the history of the Limbu people, the land of his ancestors, the spread of their "home territory," the deals made with Kathmandu rulers over the centuries and his disagreement with the way the central government was handling eastern Nepal irrespective of a democratically elected constituent assembly. Chapter 5 presents an account of some aspects of "Limbuwan" and provides background information to the political antagonism that surrounds the notion of this wished-for ethnic-based province, a contention of some Limbu parties, the largest of which sat in the assembly where Machindra was Deputy Chairman at the time.

Machindra is a republican and a democrat who engages with local, regional and national politics and administration. His goal is development for all, justice, and good governance. He could imagine and feel the peace I was talking about, yet he explained, "We are not at war any more, but we are not in peace … We don't know how to live in peace. We are not at

[87] This part of the book has been read by the Begha family for approval prior publishing, a policy that applies to the three previous case studies.

peace with Kathmandu and we are not at peace among ourselves, the Kirats … We are not at peace with one another … We need this peace."

Later in the day he would add: "I have a pain in my heart and that pain blocks my own way to peace."

This pain must be understood. It is exactly what peace requires: to understand the pain within oneself and in the other. This is empathy (towards oneself and others) – a component of the Peaceability formula. No pain should be trivialized, or brushed aside, but dealt with. Hurt and resentfulness from past practices need airing, and healing. This is part of making peace: giving authentic listening to one another's pain and, from the basis of such shared experience, finding together a new way that is mutually acceptable – be it consensus, negotiated agreement or other creative solution.

What pains Machindra and his fellow advocates of the "Limbuwan" concept is the perception and feeling of having been betrayed over centuries by a distant ruling elite composed of upper-caste Kathmandu-dwellers who, within a rigid top-down political structure and the absence of local government, *de facto* removed local political power from the hands of the inhabitants in remote regions.[88] Because Nepali citizenship was devoid of rights and meaning, many Limbu people found more pride and hope in their ethnic belongingness than in a modern sense of political self. This can be explained through the principle of substitution, especially during the propaganda of the insurgency – but it is not only that. The wide variety of ethnic identities is a tremendous richness for mankind, exemplifying human bonds with natural environments and with one another in the form of tradition, culture, spirituality, language and love of land. This has long been discussed in all countries of the world and at the United Nations, recognized in the proclamation of ethnic rights and raised to international law via the Convention concerning Indigenous and Tribal Peoples known as ILO No. 169 (1989). A key discussion in Nepal is whether, taking the ILO 169 or similar premise, such framework actually serves the Nepali people on the long-term, both in their differences and in their unity – particularly since a large mix of diverse social groups inhabits all geographic areas. And if so, in which way and to what degree? A unique Nepali answer to socio-

[88] These statements reflect the views presented by the discussion partners and not any opinion of the researcher.

political wrangles may one day provide a peaceful alternative to investing only in identity, along with the psychological freedom this may trigger.

The psychology of a native leader is often torn at times of transition. Machindra gave examples of contradictions: "We have 15 days of marriage ceremony in Kirat tradition but that is also a reason why we are not developing economically. These long rituals hold us back. Our next generation is asking us why we are losing so much time instead of attending to development matters … The types of rituals are also in conflict. One family may expect animal sacrifice while others, especially the newer generation, want to use flowers. What should I do? Sacrifice a buffalo or bring a flower? What is right? I often do not know."

Thank you, Machindra, for your honesty and care. Facing, internalizing and transforming the dilemmas at times of change is the task at hand.

### *From a Peace Park to the Peace Trail*

The next morning, I understood that Bishweshor Begha and Machindra Begha are brothers. The one has embraced community forests and has plans for tourism development; the other is a politician advocating for Limbuwan with political activists banning any actions in the forests other than those of CFUGs. The brothers may seem at times united and divided by the same one thing: their love for their people.

Here we were, sitting together in Falaicha, with Kulraj and another Limbu colleague, Nar Bahadur Mangmu, who is an expert on the region. We were discussing how to proceed with the peace park, and how to combine the objectives of the action research. It was agreed that instead of taking one ward we should take an area between two mountaintops, each place with a Pokhari (lake) of great beauty and already defined as a tourist attraction. The top of one mountain also has a rhododendron sanctuary. The potential for leisure walking and close-to-home tourism is large. To walk from Chyangthapu town to the first mountaintop, then to the second and then back to the valley takes three to four days.

Linking the hours of walking on the path from one lake (Thimbung Phokhari) to the next (Lam Pokhari) with "ecological/peace tourism" and PACE B3.i3[2], the "peace park" idea then became a "peace trail." A committee already protects cultural and religious aspects of this area and oversees the medicinal plants, herbs and animal-rearing heritage. The name of this association is Mangenalung. In cooperation with Mangenalung, we agreed to walk some of this trail together when I return the following year. But as the Great Earthquake happened, this became impossible and the project was again delayed.

This place of beauty, we must recall, also represents an apex of the conflict existing between social groups (in particular the government and ethnic communities), due to the historical disagreement over land ownership. The community forests represent a government-led program to which the Limbu people, ancestral inhabitants of these lands, say to have had no political participation at the time of their creation in the 1980s. While recognized as a beneficial scheme, it by-passes the ethnic claims and thus remains for some a point of contention. Could the peace trail become a mitigation instrument whereby opposing parties agree on the value-adding dividends of linking peace tourism with Limbu ancestral cultural and natural heritage? Can a peace trail (or any peace park), through a collective application of the Peaceability formula, itself trigger or support a synthesis of commonalities and produce a new solution? Could a peace trail act as a "third side"?[89] Could peace education contribute to resolving the endogenous social problems still hampering the full success of community forest programs?

The philosopher Hegel and the sociologist Dahrendorf have demonstrated how much the factor of recognition (or refusal of recognition) is central to social conflicts. Could a peace trail at the heart of Limbu-inhabited lands earn the full recognition of the local contribution to the national peace process, and with it the respect for the ethnic dimension?

By the time I left the Begha brothers, my imagination was running wild: a peace trail from Terai through Ilam, ending (for now) in Taplejung, via Pathibara, to reach the heart of the Kangchenjunga Peace Park. It would have been born in Panchthar with the initial trunk in Chyangthapu. A happy thought.

---

89 See William Ury, *The Third Side* (New York: Penguin Books, 2000). This is a hands-on manual on how to resolve conflict at home, at work, in the neighborhood or between communities. Ury says, "It takes two sides to fight, but a third to stop." This third side can be a person (a mediator) or it can be a thing, an event or an occasion, *e.g.*, a peace trail.

# Annex to Chapter 4
# Small Survey Conducted with and by Students at the Shree Phidim Higher Secondary School (SPHSS)

## A. Students' Survey SPHSS

1. I have observed fighting in school this year.
   Not at all Not so often Sometimes Often Much too often
2. Boys tend to harass girls.
   Not at all Not so often Sometimes Often Much too often
3. When there is a fight, teachers stop the fight.
   Not at all Not so often Sometimes Often Always
4. After a fight, teachers explain to students how to solve problems at school so that students learn appropriate behavior and conflict resolution.
   Not at all Not so often Sometimes Often Always
5. I am happy to come to school and I feel included here.
   Not at all Not very much Sometimes Much Totally
6. I observe we are at peace with each other as students and there are many friendships.
   Not at all Not very much Sometimes Much Totally
7. We are receiving explicit peace education at our school, as topics in the curriculum.
   Not at all Not so often Sometimes Often It is a central topic
8. I feel I can go and talk to my teachers if I have a problem. I can trust them and they will understand me.
   Not at all Not very much Sometimes Much Totally
9. For me, peace at school means…

## B. Teachers' Survey SPHSS

1. I have observed fighting in school this year.
   Not at all Not so often Sometimes Often Much too often
2. Boys tend to harass girls.

Not at all Not so often Sometimes Often Much too often

3. When I notice a fight or an aggressive behavior, I intervene immediately.
   Not at all Not so often Sometimes Often Always
4. After stopping inappropriate behavior, I later explain to students how to solve problems at school so that they learn civic and moral conduct for a peaceful society.
   Not at all Not so often Sometimes Often Always
5. As a teacher, I am happy to come to school. I feel included in the teachers' community and useful for the students' future.
   Not at all Not very much Sometimes Much Totally
6. When there is lack of peace at school, I think the causes are…
   a)
   b)
   c)
7. I address these causes through my profession.
   Not at all Not very much Sometimes Often Totally
8. As a teacher, I am giving explicit peace education at our school, through topics as part of the curriculum.
   Not at all Not very much Sometimes Often It is a central topic
9. If there are challenges, problems or conflicts, my colleagues and I handle these in a pro-active way. We keep a socially peaceful school environment for students and parents, thanks to our concerted conflict management measures.
   Not at all Not very much Sometimes Often Always
10. For me, peace at school means…

## C. Parents' Survey SPHSS

1. My child tells me of happy experiences at school.
   Not at all Not so often Sometimes Often Always
2. My child tells me of unhappy experiences at school
   Not at all Not so often Sometimes Often Much too often
3. I trust that the teachers will ensure that the school is a peaceful place for my child.
   Not at all Not very much Some Much Fully

4. As a parent, I support my child's learning by enquiring about school and homework.
   Not at all Seldom Sometimes Often Very much
5. I cooperate with teachers in the civic and moral education of my child (at home and at school we teach the same principles of life and learning).
   Not at all Seldom Sometimes Often Very much
6. I observe that the school is a peaceful place.
   Not at all Seldom Sometimes Often Always
7. I notice that my child is receiving explicit peace education at school, through the topics taught.
   Not at all Seldom Sometimes Often This is a central topic
8. I feel I can go and talk to the teachers and principal if I have a problem. I trust them and they will understand me as a parent.
   Not at all Not so much Sometimes Often Absolutely
9. For me, peace at school means…

## D. School Management Committee's Survey SPHSS (added only in the second round)

1. It is possible for the Shree Phidim School to live the principles and the practices of the national policy of 2011 of SZOP (Schools as Zones of Peace).
   Not at all Not so often Sometimes Very often Totally
2. I observe conflicts between groups or individuals in the school or about the school.
   Not at all Not so often Sometimes Very often Much too often
3. I observe trust and professional friendship between people related to the school.
   Not at all Not so often Sometimes Very often Always
4. As a school manager, I monitor and *control* that there is no discrimination, no sexual harassment and no corruption of any kind at the school.
   Not at all Not so often Sometimes Very often Regularly
5. A peaceful environment is necessary for educational success. Success at school is also measured by passing tests and exams. I contribute to securing peace at our school in order to secure success in exams.
   Not at all Not especially Some Much This is core to my management

6. I observe that children have peace in their mind and so may learn well.
   Not at all Not very much Some Much Totally
7. I see that teachers link the topic of peace explicitly with their subject matter.
   Not at all Not so often Sometimes Often Regularly
8. For me, sustainable peace at our school means…
   a)
   b)
9. The difficulties on the way are…
   a)
   b)
10. I contribute to surmounting the difficulties by…
    a)
    b)

# CHAPTER 5

# IN SEARCH OF THE MEANING OF LIMBUWAN, AND ITS PEACE

The connection between a people and a particular spot of land on the planet is anchored over time and in space. The expansion of an ethnic group within a geographic area and the organisation of its hierarchies, clan and family structures, ownership system, norms and traditions justify to the eyes of each generation a sense of rights and responsibilities towards the management of this territory. Of course, everyone is a descendant of some wandering tribe long ago before settlements and regulatory systems existed. Originally, we all come from somewhere else and migrated to virgin lands which we appropriated. With the advent of modernity, states were legally established through treaties between political/military powers; whether a territory was obtained by force or negotiation, it became essential to define borders that would be respected by regional neighbors and, later, recognized by international law.

As liberal Germans have recently expressed, in an attempt to redress domestic far-right xenophobia, "we are all foreigners, everywhere" (*wir sind alle Ausländer, überall*). Everywhere in the world, migrations of millions of people have taken and are taking place, continually. The reasons are multiple – some arise from positive motivations such as trying out a more promising life elsewhere, yet most are consequences of hardships as people flee war, social discrimination, political exclusion, economic stalemate or climate change.

Such is true for the Limbu people who, at different times, went to India, to Bhutan, registered as Gurkhas, signed up as migrant workers or left as large families to count among the sedentary diaspora of today. Eight million Nepali are residents of India (where half of all of remittances come from), among them many Limbus.[90] They, like the Tamang, Rai and Gurung (all

90 The census of 2011 recorded 26,494,504 people, so eight million living in India represents an extra 23.5% of Nepali people living across the southern border.

of the Kirat family) have a reputation for being excellent soldiers, who, as Gurkhas, have added much value to the British and Indian armies.

Centuries ago, Indian people had moved to Nepal to escape unfavorable changes of dynasties, find peace and cooler weather in the pre-Himalayan hills, and enjoy a liberty they could no longer have at times of upheaval or conquest. They brought the Hindu system and its caste structure with them. Assimilation – acculturation by the more structured, norm-dictating, physically taller, more entrepreneurial and Sanskrit-writing folk – happened over time. The top of the pyramid – the Brahmin closely followed by the Chhettri – connected with the center in Kathmandu more easily than the ethnic peoples of Mongolian ancestry, and a divide driven by caste, class and ethnicity gradually widened. This being said, most communities of mixed peoples (all ethnic groups, castes and classes considered), when interviewed during the study, also reported acts of solidarity, open communication and inter-group help in their multi-racial villages as being very much a way of Nepali life.

"Limbuwan," as already explained, is a territorial, historical and cultural concept that is specific to an ethnic view of identity, space and time. As with other indigenous peoples in the world, it carries a sense of ancestral belonging, an intimate relationship with the forces of nature, and close, collective social bonding. *Limbuwan* also reposes on acts and deeds from the $18^{th}$ century that guaranteed autonomy to the Limbu people by the newly centralized monarchic and military authority in Kathmandu. Practically speaking, however, it is a region inhabited by Nepali of all castes and ethnic origin, all of whom have lived there for generations and have contributed to the regional upkeep and livelihood of the eastern hills.

In Nepal today, there are 387,300 Limbu people (census of 2011) representing 1.46% of the Nepali population spread about the whole country (as are all other peoples and castes). Indeed, the nation is composed everywhere of a ubiquitous mix of Nepali of many different origins. Yet the highest density of Limbu people is found in the Mechi region, together with their close Kirat brethren, the *Rai*. The district of Panchthar has the most Limbu inhabitants (40%) and the municipality of Phidim nearly 60%. This dense presence of ethnic Kirat peoples and the openness with which I was welcomed to enter their home, witness their lifestyle and join in their cultural traditions was a deciding factor in choosing to have the study take place there.

Different geographical maps conflict in defining *Limbuwan*. While they converge to cover most of the Mechi region, some proposals vary (their authors may be Limbu or non-Limbu people). The Limbu region, however, is generally recognized as being the land of hills – lower hills, middle hills and upper hills. Many Limbu are found in the continuing hills at the foot of the Himalayas in northern India, in Darjeeling or todays' northern parts of West Bengal and in Sikkim. In Nepal, the Limbu inhabit the northern district of Taplejung but will not be as numerous in the high mountains as are the Sherpa. Due to historical migrations towards the south and a series of Limbu kingships in the Terai, there are many Limbu in the southern districts of Jhapa, Morang and Sunsari – yet they are a minority compared with indigenous people of other ancient origins.[91] To the same extent as there are many Rai in the Mechi zone, there are also many Limbu in the neighbouring Koshi zone, generally known as the ancient homeland of the Rai. The Rai and the Limbu have much in common.

There is no formal, legally recognized map of *Limbuwan*. One map is basically the Mechi region itself, covering all four districts from the Himalayas to the Indian border of the Terai (Taplejung, Panchthar, Ilam, Jhapa). Another takes the Koshi River as its western boundary and includes the districts of Terathum, Dankuta, Morang, Sunsari and part of Sankhuwasabha. A third map takes the northern areas and the hills of the Mechi and Koshi zones yet stops short of the three Terai districts (Jhapa, Morang and Sunsari), taking the lateral East-West (or Mahendra) Highway as the southern delineation – hence leaving the Terai districts to form another area.

While many Limbu people aspire to obtaining territorial recognition of their ancestral presence in eastern Nepal by having a province that carries their name within the largest possible boundary of historic reach, other Limbu people have not made this acknowledgement conditional in the recent exercise of state-building. The latter are primarily concerned that all federal states enjoy local elections and local governments, that no population group has any chance to dominate other groups in resource management or privileges, and that the federation of states guarantees a peace-enhancing equilibrium for the whole of Nepal.

---

91 Among these people are the Tharus, Rajbansis, Dhimals, Satars and others who say they were there before the "hills people" came down to dwell in the south, and who do not wish – according to several sources I met during the study – to be part of *Limbuwan*.

The difference is thus mainly between those who are liberal and want to build the whole country including their region, and those who insist on ethnic demands first. Among the latter, only some have been militant about it. This has been one area of internal divide and fragmentation post-CPA.

Based on the sampling of Limbu people taken during interviews in 2011 and 2012, less then half were adamant on *Limbuwan* as a name and a new map, while the other group would not insist on such a definition but would opt instead for an administrative province that enables rapid, pragmatic, economic development unbound to ethnic politics. All respondents cared about preserving their Limbu culture and language but many doubted whether an ethnic federal denomination was the means to achieve it. Of the non-Limbu people living in Panchthar, a few were also in favor of the *Limbuwan* agenda, while others preferred a less ethnic focus, less local emotion, more tangible actions and practical results, and more worldly awareness by the claimers themselves.

## 1. Historical Review

### *The Distant Past*

The large Kirat family has very broad origins. Some sub-families can be traced back to peoples of the Mediterranean region who migrated to Mesopotamia and the Assyrian lands in the third millennium B.C. Over time and in crossing Persia, they reached what is now northern and southern India. Many preferred the northern regions of South Asia, and, as skilled hunters, felt at ease in the hills and mountains.[92]

In traditional story-telling, however, the Kirat people of Nepal have a decidedly more northerly origin. Three groups in particular crossed or circumvented the Himal: a Chinese lineage called the Munaphens, a Mongol lineage called the Tangsangthas and the Khambos, originating from the Tibetan plateau.[93] The spread of their nomad life as well as settlements reached into the Ganges plain and today's Sikkim region. Kirat of Persian and Mongolian origins are found in today's Pakistan and Afghanistan. The Hazara people of Kabul were Kirat who, after hearing of a prosperous Indian civilization, came to see the Hindu land and then moved north. They

92 Chemjong (2003), 2–3.
93 *Ibid.*

became the Gurkhas, and, over time, adopted Hinduism. When the Aryans came and menaced the northern regions, they met with the defences of Kirat King Ashur on the Indus River. Defeated, Ashur and his people migrated to what is now Himachal Pradesh in India. Mongolian people came there too and, together, they established a strong Kirat people. In time, they moved eastwards and came to be the first rulers of Nepal.[94]

At these times, competition among faiths and rivalries among kings occurred in all directions; the early centuries B.C. in the north of Asia were largely periods of belligerence. Until the arrival of new Hindu dynasties (the first of which were the Mallas, then the Lichhavies), the Kirat lived everywhere in Nepal and strongly concentrated in what later would become the Kathmandu Valley.

### *The Middle Ages and the Unification Campaigns*

We cannot compare the arrival of northern Indian dynasties in Nepal in the 12$^{th}$-15$^{th}$ centuries with, say, the Moghul invasion of India or the colonization of 16$^{th}$-century Spaniards and Portuguese in Central and South America. Although a gradual imposition of a socio-cultural system pushed some ethnic peoples away to the northern and eastern parts of the country, a systematic change of faith "on-command," the enslaving of local populations and the exclusive exploitation of resources did not occur. The new centers of power in Bhaktapur, Lalitpur and Kathmandu shared the central but relatively limited bounty of a feudal economy among themselves (mostly in competition with one another), but they did not engage in systematic dictatorship over the native peoples who were, by and large, very difficult to reach out to.

The military campaigns of unification by Gurkha leader Prithvi Narayan Shah (1723–1775), later affirming the Shah dynasty from Kathmandu, affected the native tribes more significantly. The "Wars of Unification" were resisted by local chieftains and their armies. Yet in the lifetime of the new King Shah, truces and arrangements were made whereby the Limbu people, guided by their leaders, would be left in peace in the far eastern regions if they agreed to formally belong to the newly enlarged Nepali state and nation.

---

94 *Ibid.*, 5.

In fact, many Limbu people have, ever since, fought as defenders of central kings (as state and as Gurkha soldiers), demonstrating a heightened sense of duty towards the national identity of Nepal and its international participation.

## *The Price and Prize of Recognizing Limbuwan in the 18$^{th}$ Century*

When King Prithivi Shah[95] negotiated with the Limbu kings of the east who had united to fight against his invading Gurkha[96] troops, he agreed – in writing – to grant these rulers full independence in the management of their territory. He formally accepted to let them conduct their regional administration on the basis of the Kipat system.[97]

Two centuries followed during which the Limbu were mostly left in autonomy. They could quarrel among themselves (which they often did) or live in peace, without much intervention in their way of life from Kathmandu. Meanwhile, the rest of the country developed little in what may be seen as a belated Middle Ages, encapsulated in centralized, upper-caste politics of little radius.

One may say that unification did Nepal good by giving it a common Nepali identity, but it also came at the price of disregarding the rights of local and unique ways of life that gradually degenerated into "second-class," delocalized, ethnic and social discrimination. The centralized Hindu system based in Kathmandu did not demonstrate gender or social equality, as

95 King Prithivi Narayan Shah (1722–1775) is known as the unifier of Nepal.

96 The original Gurkha troops were the military of King Shah. For the regions that had enjoyed full autonomy until then, they represented enmity through force. Only later did the Gurkhas come to mean Nepali troops with a reputation for excellent service.

97 The Kipat is an indigenous administrative system of organizing land tenure, heritage of property, and sharing of resources among members or large families. Since the number of people was much lower at that time, ownership of a full mountainside or series of hills was not uncommon. The titles of such ownership were seldom in writing (although the Limbu language has a script, most people did not read or write). Verbal claims and oral administration were recorded in the collective understanding of chiefs and their officers, regarded as binding for all. Customary laws and codes of conduct existed and gave frameworks and guidance for societal rules. With the Kipat system, the Limbu people perceived the immense natural world around them as theirs to care for, westwards to the geographical border of the Arun River. From that river on, Nepal was now under a unifying king who would start the campaign of acculturation (Hindu religion and Nepali language, strengthening the center in Kathmandu).

groups of Dalit, women, indigenous and poor people were by default ignored by the patriarchal elites on the basis of difference.

The ancient Limbu social constellation, as is the case with most indigenous people, was a lot more egalitarian than the Hindu social system. Gender equality was also greater. This being said, Limbu history is filled with warring kings exacting endless revenge upon one another, from Taplejung to Morang. Blessed were the peaceful years when local kings united, for they were short too.

### *The Second Half of the Twentieth Century*

In 1964, King Mahendra (the ninth-generation descendent of King Prithivi Narayan Shah) was aiming to conduct campaigns of poverty alleviation, cultural transformation and educational development for his subjects. King Mahendra was aware of the "backwardness" of the citizens of Nepal, due in part to the remoteness of their dwellings and the lack of connectivity to modernity, education, markets or businesses. Witnessing the rapid transformation of India after 20 years of independence, he was keen to see such changes in Nepal too. He was also unsettled by the growing demand for grassroots politics and claims for democratic empowerment by a new generation of Nepali dissenters who were receiving republican political education in India, some it radical.

King Mahendra engaged in nationwide reforms under an umbrella program known as Panchayat. To him and his officers, the Panchayat should help uplift rural life by creating "model villages." It should also rebuke politics of dissent and replace rising voices of discontent with conservative holders of an obedient system geared towards stable and constant development. By then, however, Nepali politicians (Nepali Congress, United Marxist-Leninist, Maoists) were swelling their ranks, learning the art of opposition politics and, later, the ways of guerrilla warfare.

In his plan to modernize Nepal and create an administration in line with unilateral development programs (and also to facilitate the use of international development funds that were starting to create infrastructures in Nepal), King Mahendra and his government implemented the Land Reform Act, which de facto abolished the Kipat System of the Limbu people in the eastern lands. This was equivalent to abolishing the agreement made between King Prithivi Shah and local leaders generations before – with neither the understanding nor the consent of those concerned.

The land reform was passed with the intention to modernize, install a cadastral system, create community forests and allot land for sale for future development (water pipes, hydro-electric plants, road construction, factories and government buildings). However, many Limbu people felt that they were losing ancestral authority over their territory. The privatization as well as the nationalization of land was viewed as overly beneficial to landlords or ministerial agendas that operated from Kathmandu. This top-down decision was perceived as a betrayal and caused grievances that would later intensify the Maoist dynamics of insurgency. On the one hand, it was an understandable move towards the simplification of the Nepali system of land tenure, division, purchase and sale, and the obvious benefits of a single system involving government land and private property. On the other hand, the Limbu people felt deprived of what they had viewed for two centuries as their autonomous rights.

The violent reaction against the eradication of the Kipat system was not the first demonstration against the central powers. The *Limbuwan Autonomous Movement* had already gained in strength following the overthrow of the Rana rule.[98] On a trail of politicization by the new generation, the Limbuwan Autonomous Movement and the Limbuwan Mukti Morcha, or "Liberation Front," expressed politically the emotional resentment against what they perceived as autocratic rule. "Autonomy" was to be understood as the wish to cut the arbitrary strings to the palace in Kathmandu, and "liberation" as the desire to return to an independent *Limbuwan*. The latter party was banned from participating in the general election of 1990.

[98] The Rana was a period of political power usurped by prime ministers and ministers who *de facto* ruled Nepal for a century, debasing the rightful king to a secondary position of official protocol only. The all-powerful Jung Bahadur Rana incorporated the Hindu caste system into the civic code of Muluki Ain, together with the national policies of one language (Nepali) and one religion (Hinduism). Thus, the mother tongues of native peoples were discriminated against since they did not have any value in local administrative spoken or written language, nor were they used or taught in schools. When King Tribhuvan regained full kingly power (1951), he wanted to bring about change so that his country would be occupied by modernization and not internal strife. However, he did not undo what the Rana rulers had done constitutionally. Not did his son King Mahendra. There was too much concern for holding Nepal in firm hands and containing the new left-wing political parties.

King Birendra then justified his government's decision by agreeing that policies of autonomy – based on ethnicity and regionalism – were a threat to national sovereignty and integrity. Although King Birendra was, comparatively, a much-loved king, this statement bruised the relationship between some indigenous communities in eastern Nepal and the centralized kingly powers.

Another perspective is that of (Limbu and non-Limbu) "educated" people, including those who reside or have resided abroad and returned: they say that, "whilst Nepal is considered as very poor, Limbus generally own land, a home and animals. They have always been land-owners." Personal bankruptcy has often been the result of stringent social obligations such as extravagant dowries and wedding ceremonies. During research interviews, it was said that addiction to alcohol has prevented many Limbus from making wiser choices on how to develop their lives. During the Kipat system, it is told, much land was exchanged for the provision of alcohol. Marriages and other ceremonies at the heart of Limbu culture used to be very expensive affairs and people had to sell land to pay for the incurred debts. The educated Limbu community, NGOs, schools and the Kirat Yakthung Chumlung Association[99] are advocating for abandoning habits and social customs that are contrary to educational and economic development.

## *Recent History*

In the 1990s, the "Center" (the Kings' Courts and a burgeoning political elite) were talking at length on the benefits of a democratically elected parliament and how the country may be better-governed. Indeed, the general state of poverty and the distant, cut-off provincial structures had not changed for centuries. Modernity seemed a concept devoid of meaning to the remote regions of Nepal. The Maoist-led insurgency (1996–2006) – in

[99] The Kirat Yakthung Chumlung (KYC) is a "non-partisan and non-profit making Limbu indigenous peoples' organization established in 1989. It was registered with the government in 1990 and affiliated with the Social Welfare Council in 1994. Since its inception, it has been dedicated to the promotion and preservation of Limbu language and culture, the upliftment of socio-economic and educational condition of the Limbu people, and the consolidation of communal harmony among various communities." Its headquarters are in Lalitpur, Kathmandu, with branches overseas such as in the UK and Hong Kong. See http://chumlung.org.np, retrieved 31 May 2015. This chapter was published after the chairmanship had read and approved its content.

the name of giving egalitarian power to all – also swelled its ranks in the Limbu region as people saw a chance to access enlarged citizenship rights, reclaim their local rights (from the old Kipat system) and regain a sense of dignity.

The Maoists, using guerrilla warfare methods unknown to previous Nepali generations, impressed the youth that wanted a chance at making their own lives more successful than those of their parents. A rhetoric of social justice, gender and caste equality, empowering oneself and others, and abolishing the corruption and abuse of political powers in Kathmandu enthused millions of Nepali to consider rebellion as a credible path towards change. Many Limbu people participated in the ensuing guerrilla war, claiming that one dividend of their contribution would be the return to former local supremacy. Maoist leaders promised Limbu rebels that they would gain *Limbuwan*'s autonomy, indigenous political rights – and their land back. While this became a rallying cause, it was in fact an illegal act: the insurgents declared that the *Nun Panni ko Shanti* (Salt-Water Peace/Treaty or Gorkha-Limbuwan treaty of 1774) that had united the Limbu Area with Nepal automatically became void as a result of King Gyanendra being deposed,[100] although the arbitrary rejection of treaties was (and remains) unconstitutional. And so the claims of the Maoists and militant Limbu were not in line with national law.

Activists in Ilam say that an explicit, post-insurgency *Limbuwan* state agenda was initiated by the Chumlung office in the municipality of Ilam, in connection with representations of Limbu parties in Kathmandu. Among these groups, the Limbuwan Rastriya Mukti Morcha was basically the Maoist Limbu group, which, after the signature of the CPA, continued its demand for autonomy. The YCL (Maoists-CPN) and the Youth Force (UML) also have had a *Limbuwan* wing. Both, although claiming to advocate for *Limbuwan* concerns, were in competition as centrist parties. Often, their dispute was not in the name of the people but better resembled gang-clashes for control over resources such as forest produce, control of local markets or local "donations" (extortion, the arbitrary creation of barriers for taxes or the control of businesses such as transportation routes and vehicles). In other words, political ideology deteriorated into plain bad be-

100 King Gyanendra (reign 2001–2008), brother of the murdered King Birendra and the last king of Nepal, was deposed when Nepal became a republic.

havior by gangs of lawless youth. Immature politicking was blurring the situation and damaging the purity of the ethnic discourse. Loudly playing Limbu songs from the open windows of passenger vehicles was more a provocation than genuine nostalgia, and the revering of "martyrs" a pretext for rowdy Limbu gangs not to be brought to court for having harmed others.

Following the CPA and the election of the first Constituent Assembly (CA), the promise of ethnically autonomous provinces, announced by Maoist leaders as socio-political trophies of the People's War, was central to the debate of state-building. However, now that politicians were meeting in the chambers instead of having government and rebel armies clash in the jungle and on battlefields, it became clear that different understandings of "state reconstruction" would cause lengthy discussions embroiled by contradictions.

A potential federal reconstruction received much support across Nepal immediately. It did not, however, necessarily mean ethnic-based federal states for everyone. In fact, the search for consensus in constitution-writing was repeatedly halted mostly on the question of whether the new federation of Nepali states should be administrative or identity-based provinces.

Many Limbu were adamant that the logical outcome of fighting for a decade for their rights was to raise a new *Limbuwan* as an autonomous province, like a phoenix from the ashes. They linked the ILO No. 169 convention on the rights of indigenous peoples to their political and historically-based geographic demand. The linking of ethnic identity to the administration of national resources and political power was seen by others as dangerous for the unity of the country, inappropriate for post-modern times and potentially ineffective for a country in need of rapid development through increased Nepal-wide and regional connectivity. Equal development opportunities across all regions of Nepal regardless of caste, religious, ethnic or cultural backgrounds were also an expected peace dividend after the insurgency and seemed to contradict the aspired locally-focused ethnic-based politics.[101]

[101] Interest in ethnic politics is also present among other groups: Rai, Tamang, Tharu, Gurung, Newari (though much less adamant than with the Limbu and Madeshi communities).

## 2. Emotional Need

The *Limbuwan* idea, anchored in ethnic politics, is fed by emotions. These contain a mix of self-confidence, pride and love of place but also sadness, resentment and the fierceness to win. Some Limbu people carry grievances typical of those who, at some point in time, felt bypassed in a manner that was perceived as unjust. This wants to be heard and understood. Maybe deep listening, (*i. e.*, empathy) could lead to the emergence of new and inclusive solutions beyond the identity debate.

This emotional need resembles that of other folks in the world whose collective grievances are the product of having felt treated as second-class citizens in their own land. In many countries, the creation of a unified state and the "encroaching" of administrative powers over remote localities have led to certain disempowerment. In some regions and over time, the exclusion is deep, seemingly permanent and impossible to uproot; other times it perpetuates through emotional rhetoric while in fact circumstances have changed and new opportunities are in the making, inviting the formerly marginalized to co-create new structures and cultures that foster more positive developments.[102] Holding on to grievance may be damaging for the ones who insist on it, anchoring their pain in the next generation and maybe missing out on alternative paths to social and political peace.

## 3. Economic Need

As Nepal reveals itself to be a lot richer than could initially be supposed (waters produce electricity, quarries provide material for infrastructure, forest produce becomes exportable, tourism flourishes...), so a new generation of entrepreneurs starts to look at its own country with new eyes. Having power over one's region begins to equate to controlling its resources and managing its economy.

[102] During a focus group at Chumlung in Ilam, a politician pointed out that there had never been any government law prohibiting the use of any language or religion of nationalities in Nepal. "The Nepali language became the lingua franca of administration and education but prohibition of use of other languages never took place. Furthermore, Limbus have always been represented at central government," he said. The politician noted there were 12 recent or current Limbu ministers, including Subash Nembang, Chairman of the CA. The focus group then agreed that the Dalits had been suppressed far more than the Limbus or other Janajatis.

Whereas in the past, the economic value-adding of districts was either little or centrally managed, local populations may now increasingly consider the proximate resources as theirs to take care of, exploit and benefit from – within the legal parameters of work and industry. The soil is fertile, there is much water, and a good number of hydro-power projects of different sizes are waiting for investment and engineering. Production of, and trade in, local plants, herbs, tea and coffee are expandable. Cement and other industry – especially small cooperative-like factories – can easily be built. The road network is growing.

That local resources should be cared for by local people is the foundation of any grassroots politics and a key tenet of a federal system. While in the past inequitable systems have deprived local populations of the full fruit of their work, this is less likely to happen in a federation. Protection of the ownership of businesses (no matter the background of the business-owners) as much as control over the non-harmfulness of businesses should be guaranteed by practices of good governance everywhere, respecting corporate, labor, commercial, environmental and taxation laws.

In the past, resource conflicts have poisoned relationships between the more distant, far-flung localities and the political center. A federal system, as a matter of principle, can support more equitable cooperation between the levels of governance. Eastern hills are rich in minerals and forests, and it is now clear that an entrepreneur of any racial or societal background may step into the responsibility and personal accountability for transforming natural resources into economic value. Economic diversity should therefore thrive as a reflection of population diversity.

## 4. Limbu Spirituality

Spiritual traditions are like the rivers in Nepal: they flow strongly to a universal sea, at times running along their single beds, at times merging. The country has long been praised for its natural talent in syncretism. Diverse religious approaches have cohabited, even merged peacefully for generations. Grievances regarding the domination by the majority Hindu faith were mixed with other remonstrations during the insurgency. Since then, demands have included the right to one's own religion, pitting this demand against the Hindu ubiquity of the last centuries.[103] Today in Nepal, the freedom to choose and practice one's religion is a citizen's right, as stated in the constitution.

The Kirat religion, or Mundhum, whilst displaying some differences across sub-families, is the religion for all Kirats (Limbu, Rai, Sunuwar and Yakkha).[104] Initially animistic, it adopted much of Hinduism and Buddhism over time.

Mundhum means "the power of great strength." It is said to have existed before the Vedic Age in South Asia (c. 1500–500 B.C). Mundhum also refers to a holy script in which a cosmology of mankind and the advent of the Kirat people are written. Great myths, codes of conduct, meaningful rituals and morally-strengthening traditions must be passed down from generation to generation so as to keep on the path of truth. The Mundhum has served, until the modern times, as a guide or a source of customary laws to orientate the Kirat people in their daily lives. Devotion and chanting, worship to heal and free oneself and others from disease or other ills is a common behavior today. The Mundhum says that people should neither eat meat nor drink alcohol, and that they should honor and care for all creatures.

Though some temples (Pashupatinath, Pathibhara and others) are representative centers of the Kirat faith (next to the Hindu faith), the spiritual connection is in fact omnipresent because gods, as emanations of power, live in trees, mountain-tops, rivers and large rocks. Thus, expressions of respect are demonstrated to many elements of the natural environment.

Mythical tradition speaks of a divinity – Kirateshor – that enabled the first Kirat people to be incarnated in flesh and go about creating a peaceful civilization on earth. Due to a lack of consciousness and mistakes on their part, the Kirat people have had it more difficult (as self-made karma) than originally planned. But a well-governed life and a clear choice to do good, once reaching a critical mass, should allow for the Kirats[105] to regain this spiritual power again and fulfil their mission.

---

[103] According to the Marxist school, religion is "opium for the masses." Yet the leaders of the insurgency, many of them Brahmins, have by no means renounced their cultural attachment to religious rituals. In Nepal this is not considered a contradiction.

[104] More than 70% of the Kirati people, when asked about their religion in the census of 2011, answered "Kirat." Ten years before, it was only 30%, with almost all of the Nepali population responding "Hindu."

[105] The Kirats, Kirants or Kirati are alternative ways to speak of the Kirat people.

Through the ages, spiritual teachers, or gurus, have explained the Mundhum and guided the Kirats to live well. The first was Boli Bajo, who told of stories and myths in the Limbu language about the origins of the tribes. Boli Bajo was, it is said, an avatar or a direct incarnation of Kirateshor. Other gurus – all reincarnations of this lineage – followed. Phalgunanda was the seventh-generation avatar. His statue is at the entrance of the Phidim Gadi, next to the Mechi School.

In the lineage of gurus assuring the continuity of Kirat perennial spiritual guidance, there is today a Limbu teacher living in the hills of Ilam who is a highly respected man of knowledge and wisdom. His name is Aatmaa Nanda Lingden. He lives in an ashram from which social and educational activities are coordinated. Politicians come to see him for his wisdom and deep understanding of Nepal's search for new balance. Another Kirat guru has risen to international recognition by coining a spiritual approach called "Lovism," the central philosophy of the "Heavenly Path," which he founded at age 18. Based in Kathmandu, his name is Bhakta Kumar Rai. The spiritual teacher spent 27 hours meditating on top of Mount Everest. Today, the movement has branches in the United Kingdom, India and Bhutan, and continues to grow elsewhere in the world.

## 5. Expression of Gratitude

It was a conscious act to select the Limbu region and the Limbu people as the socio-geographic context for my study. In many places on the planet the dichotomy between international, national and local laws, between descendants of conquering migrations and native peoples, between ancient ways and modern rules are challenging humanity's collective living. The acute need for resources (water, minerals, land) bypasses concerns for ancestral land tenure or cultural rights. Economic development, more often than not, is the deciding factor. Dividing issues of modernity and structural development collide with indigenous people's view of what healthy and sustainable living is about. This is where local, national and global dimensions do not concur but conflict with one another, often times instrumentalized to serve personal interests, political agendas or economic enrichment of yet again a new (or old) elite.

My sense from the beginning is that while the discourse of *Limbuwan* became political (as all discourses have been in Nepal for the last 20 years), the bottom of the story is deeply archetypal.[106] In the sampling of the Limbu people, I was able to touch a beautiful, simple and deep connection with humanity and with the earth. The stereotypical characteristics of the Limbu people – their hospitality, family orientation, ritualistic living, cultural traditions – led me to understand their connection to the earth and their connectivity to one another. Furthermore, I observed the interplay of different levels of identity that – for the external eye – seemed in evident alignment: that of being a Limbu, a Nepali, an Asian member of humanity and a world citizen.

My interest as a peace student is that peace pedagogy enters the educational establishment right from the primary school. In childhood, it is a graceful act on the part of teachers to convey a sense of wonder and pride to be at once a descendant of an ethnic people, a Nepali national and a member of the world community. This will help develop the i3 (empathy, internal locus of control and basic trust) that in turn will empower the next generation to tackle the problems of governance and development at collective and regional (*e.g.*, South Asian) levels. Identity is an important psychological component and a strong sense of identity is conducive to consciously developing the i3. Interestingly, the stronger the i3, the less important it becomes to fight for one's identity (because it is deeply anchored in humanness and elevates beyond the parameters of genetics or socialization such as race or place).

As for the political context, the recent declaration of a Nepali Federation may well usher the Limbu people to consider their ancestral and cultural identities as a rich heritage to express to the full, leveraging some of it towards cultural, ecological and peace tourism. May they take a leap forward and help lead a strong provincial development whilst fostering a keen sense of resource management. Even if *Limbuwan* as such should not become an official political state demarcation, it can be intrinsically – and in action – a strongly beating heart of modern and post-modern advancement

[106] "Archetype" is meant in the sense of Carl Jung (1875–1921): Archetypes are common to the psyches of all humans, but each individual experiences and exhibits different characteristics in his or her own way. They are elemental forces which play a vital role in the creation of the world and of the human mind itself. In other words, the Limbu have a unique Limbu way to express humanity (as does every other culture).

for the east of Nepal. As more Limbu youth stay in the country, study in the federal province, become entrepreneurs, join in local governance and raise the local capability to regional attention, then being a Limbu may well and truly reach the aspired goals in other ways: economic development, social equity and good governance.

I take the opportunity at the end of this chapter to express my gratitude to the Limbu people who have welcomed and supported my work over the years. Right next to them, and equally helpful and kind, were the other Nepali people of all other ethnic origins and of all Hindu castes. Each and every one of them was extremely resourceful and made this adventure – and this book – possible. It is a strength of Nepal to have, as expressed in its national anthem, a "garland of flowers" symbolizing all the racial sub-families living in the country, composing its rich human tapestry. May this diversity find an enlightened approach to post-modern politics. I wish you positive breakthroughs to new levels of harmony.

My deepest thanks to all of you.

# CHAPTER 6

# MEETING THE CHALLENGES TO PEACE EDUCATION

Based on the results of surveys, interviews and focus groups in Panchthar mostly, but also in Taplejung, Ilam and Kathmandu, this final chapter aims to reflect upon some of the challenges in Nepal that have either encouraged or hindered societal evolution towards increased peace. The exercise of state-building that created the Constitution of 2015 and the establishment of a federation of seven provinces has been a rough road that has tested the patience and endurance of the population.

As if human frustrations could have an effect upon or be reflected in the natural world, the Great Earthquake of 2015 shook much of the remaining strength from the country, laying its soul bare to rely on primary survival and resilience only. How does one experience peace when one's home is gone, family members are mutilated, inflation runs wild, commodity prices rise by 50% and political factions keep on arguing violently?

How to teach peace in schools that used to be half-deserted a generation ago due to children working in the fields, that were burnt during the insurgency, that were closed through bandhs in the last decade and that finally collapsed to the ground on 25 April or 12 May 2015? The contextual conditions are extremely difficult. Yet the task remains: to build and develop Nepal.

There are indicators that Nepal is going to do better than before. The country is indeed developing despite or because of such challenges. Nepal has gone through a tremendous amount of learning in the last 30 years. The question is: Must one always learn through pain? Is it possible to learn through peace, poise, reconciliation and the management of resources based on federal governance? Can Nepal resolve its intrapersonal conflicts and emerge as a good mediator between its multi-stakeholders? There is no reason why not.

Discussing these questions and proposing peace pedagogies as national strategies, this chapter also recommends their use and transferability to other regions of the world, including Europe.

## 1. Challenges to Peace Education in Nepal

We cannot say that the challenges to peace education in Nepal are purely economic in nature. It is not because of lack of funds that peace is not central to the curriculum in schools and universities. We cannot link it to environmental difficulties either: the landscape, the weather or the lack of particular resources are not responsible for teaching more or less peace in formal and informal education. We also cannot connect the challenges to social factors: all Nepali people of all origins long for peace, deserve peace and will perfectly understand the intellectual and practical advantage of having peace as an explicit foundation of their national education.

The main factor for not making peace central to education may be political. It seems as if the presence of peace is interpreted as leading some sub-groups to win and others to lose, as if peace was going to force parties and individuals to compromise and hence lose face, to abandon battles, to miss out on personal opportunities, to reduce clan supremacy and thus to reduce power. This is a fundamental misjudgement of what peace is about, and it explains the relatively modest successes of the Peace Ministry inasmuch as it fully depends on peaceful politics being made by leaders. The challenge to peace pedagogy is a political misconception of the nature and potential outcomes of peace, which is misconstrued as weakness or potential loss of power.

## 2. Disputes

Having spent hours interviewing highly-ranked individuals from various ministries, political parties and large organizations in eastern Nepal and in Kathmandu, I have come to respect their genuine desire to serve their country. Their rhetoric is often remarkably the same – no matter their allegiance – as they all want to serve a New Nepal.

I have also observed the disingenuous last-minute events and triggers by which a likely positive development of an issue towards compromise and mutual agreement on a Monday is suddenly severed and cancelled on the Tuesday, because of some trivial item that is given scandal-like importance and thus breaks the deal in an atmosphere of despondency (or so it seems to my limited vantage point). Two weeks later, a rapprochement can again seem to be found, only to be once more dismantled at short notice.

The media is occupied trying to make sense of such to-ing and froing, searching for importance in what may not necessarily really require national attention. This unfortunately diverts the analytical capacity of intelligent citizens who start shying away from the otherwise extraordinarily interesting and significant exercise of nation-and-state-building.

No one in particular can be blamed for this. In fact, there is no blame. This is just a simple observation that these are habitual, cultural ways of navigating disagreement. They are embedded in the political process.[107] While grassroots peaceful transformation occurs via civil society and the diligent work performed by NGOs in service to remote populations, a high-level acculturation to peace politics would be welcome as an equivalent, mirroring necessity.

That Nepali people are by nature peaceful is an understatement; it has always been a prominent feature observed by foreigners ever since we had access to travel the South-Asian base of the Himalayas. This culturally embedded peace is an asset. The leadership is responsible for banking on this social capital, and for demonstrating its traditional conflict-resolution capability by aligning local and national goals under one strong principle: sustainable development to deliver social equity via good governance. When it does, then school teachers and university professors will teach in peaceful ways the disciplines that are relevant for the professionalization of the students in their participation towards building a country at peace.

## 3. The Great Earthquake

On 25 April, the day of the Great Earthquake in 2015, I was working in Nepal. In response to the disaster, NGOs from Europe called me to coordinate with Nepali NGOs the spending of aid money on emergency items. One year later, these same NGOs continue to support the reconstruction of buildings, mostly schools and village community centers.

The insurgency had claimed over 17,000 lives. Ten years of political disputes saw continued violence. On 25 April and again on 12 May 2015,

[107] This is true of all countries and governments with more or less theatrical capability. Some are characterized by political orientations linked to religion or by the historically petrified duality of Democrats vs. Republicans (USA), Conservative vs. Labor (UK), or other specificities based on opposition and dispute rather than collaboration and dialogue.

the earth shook to cause another 9,000 deaths and 21,000 injured victims.[108] Countless houses and public buildings, especially in the 14 most affected districts, were shaken to the ground, leaving 3.5 million people homeless. The disaster has been recorded as the worst in Nepal's history in terms of human casualties with one in three Nepali being affected, one in ten having become homeless and half a million households having lost their livelihoods. It is the poor – the subsistence farmers – that are the most affected.

In rankings of the world's countries, Nepal is listed as the 11th most vulnerable to earthquakes and the 30th to flood risks. Much of the population of Nepal is vulnerable to an ever-present combination of various natural dangers, ranking the yountry second in the world for the risk of mortality from two or more hazards. "Nearly 80 percent of our geographic area is at risk from multiple natural hazards, with the vast majority of our population inhabiting these high-risk areas. The recent earthquake sequence was a wake-up call to all of us," according to Ram Sharan Mahat.[109]

An International Consortium had been formed in May 2009 to support the Government of Nepal in developing a long-term Disaster Risk Reduction Action Plan. This plan was the expansion and further application of the National Strategy for Disaster Risk Management.[110] "The Consortium initiated a multi-stakeholder participatory process with the Government of Nepal and civil society organizations to identify short to medium-term disaster risk reduction priorities that are both urgent and viable within the current institutional and policy arrangements in the country."[111]

In line with the successive three-year development plans, Nepal's coun-

---

[108] Nepal Disaster Risk Reduction Portal created by the Government of Nepal, retrieved 20 May 2015. The data refers to 25 April and 12 May, both large tremors of 7.8 and 7.3 on the Richter scale respectively. The total value of structural losses has been estimated at US $10 billion.

[109] See Mahat (2015). Ram Sharan Mahat is a former Finance Minister of Nepal.

[110] Members of the Consortium are the Asian Development Bank (ADB), the International Federation of the Red Cross and Red Crescent Societies (IFRC), United Nations Development Programme (UNDP), UN Office for the Coordination of Humanitarian Affairs (OCHA), UN International Strategy for Disaster Reduction (ISDR) and the World Bank. See: http://www.adrc.asia/countryreport/NPL/2011/FY2011B_NPL_CR.pdf, retrieved 26 April 2016.

[111] *Ibid.*

try strategies had been geared to include risk prevention in all projects (road building, excavations, energy plants, land use planning, urban development, monitoring and evaluation of structures, etc.). All structures should be built with a capacity to withstand earthquakes, landslides and floods, within the context of a master plan that helps divert and reduce such hazards. The twelfth three-year development plan had set its disaster management goal to be achieved in alignment with the goals of the Hyogo Framework for Action by 2015[112] – towards a disaster-resilient Nepal. Mainstreaming disaster risk reduction, institutional and legal reform and preparedness for better response were the strategies of this plan[113] – and still are.

As the tectonic plates collided at the base of the Himalayas, the shaking of the earth took no notice of such plans. Reality on the ground was like a castle of cards blown by the wind, and the immediate disaster recovery came through the rapid mobilization of hundreds of thousands of Nepali people who showed tremendous solidarity in action. The world community, disaster-relief professionals, friendly governments, international NGOs, aid and development agencies, countless foreign groups and individuals contributed to the immediate alleviation of pain and to long-term rebuilding. Most of these efforts will continue for some years to come.

The shock of utter loss was followed by more hardships: the banning of tending the fields for fear of renewed trembling; subsistence living in camps or makeshift huts through the rainy season and the cold winter; the confusing riots against the new federal constitution and the burning of public buildings in the south (a part of the country mostly untouched by the earthquake) while in the hills of the north the people would have dreamed to still be enjoying their public spaces; the price hikes of commodities due to a five-month long border closure (triggered by the politically-driven riots close to India),[114] hindering the procurement and transportation of con-

---

[112] See The World Conference on Disaster Reduction, 2005, Kobe, Hyogo, Japan, http://www.unisdr.org/2005/wcdr/intergover/official-doc/L-docs/Hyogo-framework-for-action-english.pdf, retrieved 26 April 2016.

[113] *Ibid.*, 12.

[114] Interpretations for India to close the border vary, e.g.: 1) protection against the riots at its border; 2) forcing the government of Nepal to give more power to the southern state of the new federation because of the proximate connection with it. This area is mostly inhabited by the Madeshi, who have close ties with India and have claimed for a larger and more autonomous federal province than that which was decided under the new constitution.

struction materials; the lingering hold on administrative go-ahead to start rebuilding as a consequence of delayed strategic and operational planning at the central and local levels.[115]

The Great Earthquake surely was a challenge to education too. Schools were destroyed, pupils and students or their family members were hurt, and the Ministry of Education postponed the reopening of establishments until only after buildings could be declared as safe or temporary building erected.

The disappearance of homes and schools is a radical hindrance to education, but not to peace education. For peace education does not happen sitting on school benches. Communities that help each other – this is peace education. Responding to need no matter the people's backgrounds – this is peace education. Friendly governments pledging to help rebuild – this is conducive to peace education.

The coming together of innovative, older, experienced people and younger, fresh minds to design new villages, with new systems for heating and water circulation and earthquake-resistant structures built with environmentally friendly materials and culture-respecting architecture – this too is peace education. The blending of personal, communal, national and international funds to build the next wave of ecologically sound "model villages," blending the wish for modernity and the love of tradition – this also is peace education. The non-corrupt administration of money that flows into projects which are planned, applied and evaluated by the people and for the people – this certainly is peace education. And afterwards, we can go back to university and transform this giant natural experiment into theories of peace-building in post-conflict, post-disaster frameworks of heavily traumatised but otherwise extraordinarily beautiful and resilient societies.

## 4. Schools as Zones of Peace – Responding to the Challenges

The challenges elucidated above are only but aspects of a more complex, historical, socio-economic tapestry of circumstances and events that make

[115] Families who are victims of the earthquake received US $145 for emergency items, the first installment of a total benefit payment with a promised value of US $1,850 to help rebuild their homes. By April 2016, the full benefit payments had reached only a few of the families, mostly those who live in the mountainous areas where tourists come. Tourism, the second income sector after overseas remittances, normally brings about US $11.5 million in revenue, but it fell in 2015 by 32% as a result of the earthquake.

up the personality and current development stage of Nepal. As with every person and every group or nation, it reflects both the internal capacity to transform things for the better (internal locus of control) and the impact of surrounding forces upon a people (external locus of control). In an effort to find peace-focused responses to these challenges, the following paragraphs discuss actions already started in Nepal today and the necessity for them to expand and deepen. They are all pedagogical in nature.

We have presented SZOP in Chapters 1 and 2 and now aim to imagine an expansion of this policy. It was made public by the Department of Education in 2011 and since then has been supported by UNICEF, UNESCO, the Peace Fund, Save The Children and many other international and national entities, large and small.

SZOP is a primary program, a key driver towards the advent of societal peace in Nepal. When pupils and students are taught the meaning and practice of consensus, mutual problem-solving, inter-communal equity and political dialogue, and are given the psychological foundation for self-esteem and belief in the positive impact of one's deeds, then the next generation will be capable of turning strife into accord, obstacles into opportunities and poverty into abundance.

As in all systems and organizations, the top reflects the bottom and vice-versa. Peaceability is a competence, a capability, and it has to emanate from the Department of Education, the designers of the national curriculum, the creators of local curricula in ethnic languages, the training of teachers, the tertiary university courses for future teachers, the upskilling of education officers, the good governance of school management committees and the pertinent feedback of education auditors. It is a four-pronged strategy: 1) teaching peacefully; 2) teaching the topic of peace in diverse manners for different ages; 3) embedding peace as a driver throughout all administrative, functional and operational aspects of national education; 4) following through on the impact of peace education in schools over time and across the country. The latter presupposes a comprehensive engagement in auditing, research and evaluation according to pre-defined peace criteria.

SZOP, to become "best practice," needs to enter the culture at its deepest level, consciously and unconsciously. Peace has been forever present, albeit a peace of submission, of simplicity due to lack of choice and of natural life that was often more akin to subsistence and survival. Then there was war, a breach of the old peace, a painful awakening to realities and bad practices that had gone ignored for too long. Now, there have been ten years of sorting through what happened, why it happened and what to do next. The sorting goes on, unabated by the disastrous earthquake of 2015.

The search for a new paradigm of peace for the Himalayan Republic is probably the most sense-making synthesis of the incredible tos-and-fros of all social groups as they take two steps forward to unite and one step back to highlight divergences, regain autonomy and re-bank on personal power. But if we are to look at the "big picture," even in the wake of a terrible natural disaster, we see improvement, shared intelligence, energetic use of liberties, entrepreneurship, and a lot more qualitative education. Nepal did not fall back into civil conflict but continued building capacities after the departure of the UNMIN[116], maintaining its course towards a new constitution with a federal structure. Many may despair at the length of time it has taken or the imperfections it has entailed,[117] but it has materialized. It is the task of politicians, also, to make bold decisions that slice through the tos-and-fros, and that are sometimes unpopular. The earthquake pushed for such a decisive handling and so it came about.

Now is the perfect time for schools to move to the next phase of SZOP. Less in need of protection from external violence, classrooms can become intellectual and emotional sanctuaries and laboratories where children and students learn about and reflect upon the peace factor that potentially drives through the new federal definition of their country. Their teachers can help them awake to their responsibility in turning this potential into reality.

As schools are rebuilt after the earthquake, it is a pertinent occasion to declare the new buildings SZOP and to allow peace to enter the culture of school life, home life and village life.[118] Peace pedagogy, by becoming a key tenet of the education strategy, develops into "best practice" that gradually becomes a national competence.[119] Nepali students, professionals and lay

---

[116] United Nations (Political) Mission in Nepal (2007–2011).

[117] Ethnic-based political parties disagree on the formation of the current federative provinces, in particular the Madhesi province in the south.

[118] This is what was done in Phidim, Panchthar: with donors from Germany, one school to date has been rebuilt. The promise and engagement by the villagers to help rebuild the school and to declare it a Zone of Peace have been fully demonstrated. The local supervision was conducted by the NGO Alternative Energy Development Centre, in Phidim (2015 and 2016). A second school is in discussion at the time of writing, linking the donation with the government policy of SZOP – in all its practical aspects.

[119] US economist Michael E. Porter, an eminent author and professor on management, has

people are keen debaters and can engage in state-of-the-art dialog methodologies. These skills will be needed as the practical functionalities of federalism enter local politics, administrations and organizations. Nepal's capability to manage this next step – on the basis of constructive, pragmatic peace – can both benefit the Nepali people and serve as an example to other nations and regions of the world.

---

developed the concept of "national competitiveness," which observes how countries and regions develop produce, products, services or know-how that are unique to their physical spaces and histories, and combine to create an agent of growth or a condition for resilience at times of crises. See Porter (1990).

# CONCLUSION

Over a decade of teaching and conducting social and peace studies in Nepal and despite the relative shortness of each of the thirteen visits (between three and seven weeks at a time), I have been continuously and increasingly confident that the multilingual, multi-ethnic and multi-religious Himalayan Republic is a very positive example of a country diligently working on transforming weaknesses and problems into strengths and solutions.

November 2016 is the tenth anniversary of the Comprehensive Peace Agreement. Despite – or even because of – political strains, discord regarding the initial federative provinces, the long way to a resilient national economy and the tremendous blow by the recent earthquake, the Nepali people hold together and demonstrate community spirit in (re)building a better future.

This study was dedicated to the anchoring of interconnecting peace systems via Schools as Zones of Peace. Beyond this, it sought to observe, understand and interpret the perceptions of campus students in the far-east. Formal and informal educational establishments, dignitaries, civil society and the population at large all proved to be genuinely interested and desirous to contribute. This allows me to conclude with a word of invitation for other peace researchers to continue such action-research with school pupils and university students, cross-checking their statements against policies and facts in towns and villages.

For those who enjoy small-scale experiments, they may wish to take the PACE formula and deepen our understanding of the causal relations between individual peace-proneness and collective achievements towards a fairer society. Psychologists and educationalists may devise research designs and questionnaires to test, expand or specify *empathy*, *locus of control* and *basic trust* in the peaceability of children, youth and adults. Economists and political scientists may formulate new dimensions, criteria or measuring tools to gauge *social equity*, *good governance* and *sustainable economic development*. I wish them all the best in blending intuition with rational and critical thinking, for the realization of more peaceful systems.

"Peace," as my professor Wolfgang Dietrich (Innsbruck University) once said, "… is for heroes." I think he meant that it takes courage to choose peace again and again, above all else, at times of rest and especially at times of unrest. Peace is hard work because the only real instrument that will have the chance to act and have an impact as leverage between forces is *oneself*. Nothing else.

Peace, we have reiterated, is a capability – an attribute. It is a moral, mental, emotional, social, spiritual, ethical, human strength. It is learnable. This study was meant as a small contribution to deciphering elements of such attributes at individual and societal levels. I have learned many lessons on the way and invite my friends and colleagues in the peace education community to (critically, and I am sure they will) build upon it.

To my Nepali friends and colleagues, please do not despair at the fragility of your homeland. Tough lessons are for the best students, and Nepal has gone through an enormous amount of learning since the turn of the millennium. The cohesiveness of the Nepali folk-soul is strong, akin to some form of ancestral *basic trust*. It is being called forth to come to the surface and to state its cultural and national entity. State mentors and leaders owe it to this and the next generation to affirm outwardly the unity that exists inherently.

One day, maybe, citizens of formerly rich countries will come and beg asylum in the coolness of the Nepali hills and mountains. I often gave this scenario during focus groups to then enquire about the respondents' reactions; they always said, unanimously: "Welcome, we will help you." Maybe this is a fantasy, yet it would once again, in the revolving turns of history and civilizations, prove the adage that "the last will be first."

In the meantime, my heartfelt thanks to the Nepali people who have long understood that the "Zone of Peace" lies first in their hearts, expands in their relations with each other, and then can be expressed in their systems of governance. The anthem tells this most clearly:

Woven from hundreds of flowers, we are one garland that is Nepali
Spread sovereign from Mechi to Mahakali.
A playground for nature's wealth unending
Out of the sacrifice of our braves, a nation free and unyielding.
A land of knowledge, of peace, the plains, hills and mountains tall
Indivisible, this beloved land of ours, our motherland Nepal.
Of many races, languages, religions, and cultures of incredible sprawl
This progressive nation of ours, all hail Nepal.

# BIBLIOGRAPHY


Adelman, I. (1961). *Theories of Economic Growth and Development*. Stanford: Stanford University Press.

Adhikari, S.K. (2013). "Economic implication of Co-operative movement with reference to agriculture of Nepal." https://withagriculture.wordpress.com/tag/cooperative-movement-in-nepal/

Ali, S.H., ed. (2007). *Peace Parks*. Cambridge, Mass.: MIT Press.

Barbarin, O., and Richter, L. (2001). *Mandela's Children: Growing up in a Post-Apartheid South Africa.* New York: Routledge.

Bartelmus, P. (2008). "Indicators of Sustainable Development." The Encyclopedia of Earth. http://www.eoearth.org/article/Indicators_of_sustainable_development

Becker, B. (1997). *Sustainability Assessment: A Review of Values, Concepts, and Methodological Approaches.* Washington, D.C.: World Bank.

Besançon, M. (2003). *Good Governance Rankings: The Art of Measurement*. Boston: World Peace Foundation.

Bhattarai, A.M. (2014). "Community Forest Management in Nepal and the Judiciary." http://www.asianjudges.org/wp-content/uploads/2014/09/Community-Forest-Management-in-Nepal-and-the-Judiciary.ananda.pdf, retrieved 29 December 2015.

Boston, J. *et al*. (2010). *Public Policy: Why Ethics Matter*. Canberra: ANU Press.

Brenman, M. (2010). "Equity Impact Assessment." http://www.ewu.edu/Documents/CBPA/NWTTAP/2010_Symposium/Presentations/EquitIimpactAssessSocialEquityAnalysis.pdf. Retrieved 19 March 2016.

Chemjong, I.S. (2003). *History and Culture of Kirat People*. Lalitpur: Kirat Yakthung Chumlung.

Chemonics (2006). "Job Creation and Employability in Jordan: Survey Methodology Design Support." http://www4.hrsdc.gc.ca/gl.4ss.1ry@-eng.jsp?wrd=Participation+in+Political+Activities&iid=68

Collier, P. (2007). *The Bottom Billion: Why the Poorest Countries are Failing and What Can Be Done About It*. New York: Oxford University Press.

Corfee-Morlot, J., Kamal-Chaoui, L., Donovan, M.G., Cochran, I., Robert, A., and Teasdale, P.J. (2009). *Cities, Climate Change and Multilevel Governance*. Paris: OECD.

Deutsche Welle (2015). "Dalai Lama on Paris attacks: ‚Work for peace, and don't expect help from God and governments.'" http://www.dw.com/en/dalai-lama-on-paris-attacks-work-for-peace-and-dont-expect-help-from-god-and-governments/a-18852858

Duquesne, I. (2011). *Nepal, Zone of Peace*. Paris: L'Harmattan; Kathmandu: Bhrikuti Academic Publications.

Endicott, K. (2013). "Peaceful Foragers. The significance of the Batek and Moriori for the question of innate human violence," in *War, Peace and Human Nature. The Convergence of Evolutionary and Cultural Views*. Ed. Fry, D. Oxford: Oxford University Press.

Frederickson, H.G. (2010). *Social Equity and Public Administration: Origins, Developments and Applications.* New York: M.E. Sharpe.

Gonzalez-DeHass, A.R., and Willems, P.P. (2013). *Theories in Educational Psychology: Concise Guide to Meaning and Practice*. Lanham, Md.: R&L Education.

Hartmeyer, H. (2008). *Experiencing the World: Global Learning in Austria – Developing, Reaching Out, Crossing Borders*. Münster: Waxmann.

ILO (2012). "Key Indicators of the Labour Market." http://kilm.ilo.org/KILMnetBeta/default2.asp

International Institute for Sustainable Development (2011). "Compendium: A Global Directory to Indicator Initiatives." http://www.iisd.org/measure/compendium/DisplayInitiative.aspx?id=153

Jaffee, D. (1998). *Levels of Socio-Economic Development Theory*. 2nd ed. Westport, Ct.: Praeger.

Johnson, N., and Svara, J. (2011). *Justice for All: Promoting Social Equity in Public Administration*. New York: M.E. Sharpe.

Kalat, J. (2011). *Introduction to Psychology.* Belmont: Wadsworth, CENGAGE Learning.

Lloyd K. (2008). "An Analysis of Maria Montessori's Theory of Normalization in Light of Emerging Research in Self-Regulation." PhD dissertation, Oregon State University, UMI 3326413.

Mahat, R.S. (2015). "Toward a Resilient Nepal," in "End Poverty in South

Asia." World Bank, http://blogs.worldbank.org/endpovertyinsouthasia/toward-resilient-nepal, retrieved 26 April 2016.

Marsh, H. W., and Richards, G. E. (1986). "The Rotter Locus of Control Scale: The comparison of alternative response formats and implications for reliability, validity and dimensionality." *Journal of Research in Personality*, 20, 509–558.

Marsh, H. W., and Richards, G. E. (1987). "The multidimensionality of the Rotter I-E Scale and its higher order structure: An application of confirmatory factor analysis." *Multivariate Behavioral Research*, 22, 39–69.

Maslow, A.H. (1943). "A Theory of Human Motivation." *Psychological Review*, 50, 370–396.

Nixon, J., and Weiss, M. (2011). "Sustainable Economic Development Strategies." Global Urban Development (GUD). http://www.globalurban.org/Sustainable_Economic_Development_Strategies.pdf

OECD (2007). *Glossary of Statistical Terms.* http://stats.oecd.org/glossary/detail.asp?ID=7237, retrieved 14 March 2016.

OECD (2007). "Recent Trends and Regulatory Implications in Socially Responsible Investment for Pension Funds." 2007 OECD Roundtable on Corporate Responsibility. http://www.oecd.org/dataoecd/3/0/38550550.pdf

Page, J. (2008). *Peace Education: Exploring Ethical and Philosophical Foundations.* Charlotte: Information Age Publishing.

Porter, M.E. (1990). "The Competitive Advantage of Nations" *Harvard Business Review*, March-April, 73–91.

Rotter, J.B. (1966). "Generalized expectancies for internal versus external control of reinforcement." *Psychological Monographs*, 80.

Rotter, J.B. (1954). *Social Learning and Clinical Psychology*. New York: Prentice-Hall.

Rawls, J. (1971). *A Theory of Justice*. Cambridge, Mass.: Harvard University Press.

Rothbaum, F., Weisz, J.R. and Snyder, S.S. (1982). "Changing the world and changing the self: A two-process model of perceived control." *Journal of Personality and Social Psychology*, 42 (1), 5–37.

Sakya, K. (2014). *All the best*. Kathmandu: Buddha Maya Publications.

Schmuck, R. (2006). *Practical Action Research for Change. Thousand Oaks*, Corwin Press.

Soubbotina, T. (2004). *Beyond Economic Growth: An Introduction to Sustainable Development*. 2nd ed. Washington, D.C.: World Bank.

Spreng, N., McKinnon, M., Mar, R. and Levine, B. (2009). "The Toronto Empathy Questionnaire: Scale development and initial validation of a factor-analytic solution to multiple empathy measures." *Journal of Personality Assessment*, 91, 62–71.

Sustainable Europe Research Institute (2008). "Methods and Tools for Integrated Sustainability Assessment (MATISSE)." http://www.matisse-project.net/projectcomm/

Todaro, M., and Smith, S. (2009). *Economic Development*. Harlow: Pearson.

UN (2001). "Indicators of Sustainable Development." http://www.un.org/esa/sustdev/publications/indisd-mg2001.pdf

UNESCO (2005). "e-Governance Capacity Building." http://portal.unesco.org/ci/en/ev.php-URL_ID=5205&URL_DO=DO_TOPIC&URL_SECTION=201.html, retrieved 14 March 2016.

Uwazie, E.E. (2003). *Conflict Resolution and Peace Education in Africa*. Lanham, Md.: Lexington Books.

World Bank (2007). "Social Exclusion and the EU's Social Inclusion Study." http://siteresources.worldbank.org/INTECONEVAL/Resources/SocialExclusionReviewDraft.pdf

Ziviler Friedensdienst (2010). *Wir scheuen keine Konflikte*. Göttingen: Rüdiger Wolff.